AF488382

Nebula Nexus
(Monochrome Edition)

Knox

Copyright © 2024 Knox

All rights reserved.

ISBN: 9798339914099

Table of Contents

Chapter 1
1
The Cosmic Web

Chapter 1: Understanding the Vast Unknown

Standing at the Edge of Infinity

There is a special kind of quiet that descends when you find yourself far from the noise of civilization, beneath a night sky that stretches infinitely in all directions. It's a moment of stillness, when the chatter of everyday life fades, and you are left with only the stars above and your thoughts. The sky, a deep, velvet-black canvas, is punctuated by points of light—stars, planets, galaxies—each a reminder of the vastness that surrounds us. And in that moment, standing there under the blanket of the cosmos, you might feel a sensation that is both humbling and empowering: you are a part of this universe, a tiny but conscious piece of the grandest puzzle.

The sheer scale of the universe is difficult to comprehend. Our planet, Earth, is a small rock orbiting an average-sized star, which itself is just one of billions in the Milky Way galaxy. And the Milky Way is just one galaxy among billions, maybe even trillions, spread across the observable universe. The distances between these galaxies are so vast that they are measured not in kilometers or miles but in *light-years*—the distance light travels in one year, roughly 9.46 trillion kilometers. Light from the nearest star to our Sun, Proxima Centauri, takes 4.24 years to reach us. The light from some of the more distant galaxies takes billions of years to arrive, meaning that when we observe them, we are looking at them as they were billions of years ago.

This brings us to one of the most profound truths of our existence: when we look at the night sky, we are not just seeing distant objects.

We are looking back in time. The farther we peer into the cosmos, the further back in time we go, observing the universe in its various stages of evolution. Every star we see, every galaxy we observe, is a glimpse into the past.

But this, too, is limited. What we call the "observable universe" is only a small part of the whole. Beyond what we can see, there may lie regions of space and time that remain forever beyond our reach, hidden by the limits of the speed of light and the expansion of the universe. These unseen regions raise one of the greatest questions of cosmology: what lies beyond the observable horizon? Is there more universe out there, or does the universe curve back on itself, creating a zero?

The Observable Universe: A Window to the Past

The observable universe is like a bubble around us, with a radius of about 46.5 billion light-years. Within this bubble, we can detect light that has had time to travel to us since the beginning of the universe, roughly 13.8 billion years ago. This bubble defines our cosmic horizon—everything beyond it is out of reach, as the light from those regions has not yet had time to reach us.

Within this observable universe are billions of galaxies, each containing billions or even trillions of stars. But the observable universe is just a fraction of the whole. The universe itself could be much larger—possibly infinite. Some cosmologists speculate that what we see is just a tiny region of a much larger structure, and that the universe beyond our observable bubble might be very different. There could be regions where the laws of physics vary, or where the fundamental constants that govern the universe are slightly different.

This idea gives rise to the concept of the *multiverse*, which we will explore in later chapters.

But for now, our focus remains on what we can see—the observable universe, a vast but finite window into the cosmos.

The Cosmic Web: The Universe's Hidden Structure

When we look at galaxies spread across the universe, we don't see a random distribution. Instead, they are arranged in a vast, intricate structure known as the *cosmic web*. This web is composed of filaments of dark matter, gas, and galaxies, stretching across hundreds of millions of light-years. At the intersections of these filaments are clusters of galaxies, while in between the filaments lie enormous voids, regions of space almost entirely empty.

The cosmic web is a beautiful and complex structure, one that challenges our understanding of the universe's formation. How did such a grand design come into being? To answer this, we need to travel back to the very beginning—the Big Bang.

From the Big Bang to the Cosmic Web

The universe began as a singularity—a point of infinite density and temperature. In the first fraction of a second after the Big Bang, the universe underwent an extraordinary expansion, known as *cosmic inflation*. During this period, the universe grew exponentially, smoothing out any irregularities and creating the nearly uniform cosmos we see in the cosmic microwave background radiation (CMB), the afterglow of the Big Bang.

But this uniformity didn't last. Small quantum fluctuations in the density of matter were stretched by inflation, and over billions of years, these fluctuations grew under the influence of gravity. Regions with slightly more matter attracted more matter, and over time, these regions became the filaments and clusters of galaxies that make up the cosmic web.

As the universe cooled, particles formed atoms, and gravity began pulling matter together. The first stars ignited, galaxies formed, and the cosmic web took shape. This process is ongoing—galaxies continue to move, pulled by the gravitational forces of the web, and the universe continues to expand.

Dark Matter and Dark Energy: The Universe's Invisible Forces

One of the most fascinating discoveries of the 20th century was that the matter we can see—stars, planets, gas, and dust—makes up only a small fraction of the universe's total mass-energy content. About 85% of the matter in the universe is *dark matter*, an invisible substance that does not emit, absorb, or reflect light. We can't see it directly, but we know it exists because of its gravitational effects on galaxies.

Without dark matter, the cosmic web would not exist. It is dark matter's gravitational pull that shaped the large-scale structure of the universe. But what exactly is dark matter? Despite decades of research, we still don't know. It could be composed of as-yet-undiscovered particles, or it might represent something entirely new in our understanding of physics.

Even more mysterious is *dark energy*, a force that makes up about 68%

of the universe's total energy. Discovered in the late 1990s, dark energy is responsible for the accelerating expansion of the universe. While gravity pulls matter together, dark energy pushes it apart, driving galaxies away from each other at an ever-increasing rate.

Dark matter and dark energy are two of the greatest mysteries in cosmology. Together, they shape the universe on the largest scales, and yet, we know almost nothing about their true nature. They are reminders that even with all our scientific advancements, the universe still holds many secrets.

Analogies and Imagination: Making Sense of the Vast Unknown

To grasp the scale and complexity of the universe, it helps to use analogies:

- **Raisin Bread**: Imagine a loaf of raisin bread baking in the oven. As the dough rises, the raisins (representing galaxies) move farther apart from each other. This is a simplified model of how the universe expands. The galaxies are not moving through space; space itself is expanding, carrying the galaxies with it.
- **A Spider's Web**: The cosmic web can be thought of as a spider's web, with galaxies clustering at the intersections of filaments. Just as a spider's web is delicate yet strong, the cosmic web connects galaxies across immense distances, binding them together through the force of gravity.
- **Jellyfish in the Ocean**: Picture dark matter as the ocean and galaxies as jellyfish floating within it. The ocean (dark matter)

is invisible to someone who can only see the jellyfish (galaxies), but it shapes their movement and distribution.

The Quest for Knowledge: Science and Spirituality

S0cience has given us incredible tools to explore the universe. Through telescopes, satellites, and particle accelerators, we can observe the cosmos in wavelengths of light invisible to the human eye, from radio waves to X-rays. We can measure the temperature of the universe just a few hundred thousand years after the Big Bang, and we can peer into the hearts of distant galaxies.

But while science explains *how* the universe works, it often leaves unanswered the deeper questions of *why* the universe exists, or what its ultimate purpose might be. This is where philosophy and spirituality come in, offering a different lens through which to view the cosmos.

Many spiritual traditions teach that the universe is more than just a physical space—it is a creation imbued with meaning and purpose. Whether we call this higher power God, Brahman, or the Divine, the idea that the universe is a manifestation of a greater consciousness resonates with many.

Science and spirituality are often seen as opposing forces, but they can also complement each other. Science reveals the beauty and complexity of the universe, while spirituality explores its deeper significance. Together, they provide a more complete understanding of the cosmos.

Embracing the Mystery

The more we learn about the universe, the more we realize how little we truly know. Each discovery leads to new questions, and each answer reveals new mysteries. This is the beauty of exploration—the journey is never-ending, and the possibilities are infinite.

The universe invites us to wonder, to question, and to seek understanding. It challenges us to push the boundaries of our knowledge and to embrace the unknown. Whether through the lens of a telescope or the introspection of the mind, we are explorers on a voyage of discovery.

Conclusion: A Journey Begins

As we stand on the threshold of the universe, looking out into the vast unknown, we are reminded of the profound mystery that surrounds us. The cosmos is both larger and more complex than we can possibly imagine, and yet, we are intimately connected to it. The atoms in our bodies were forged in the hearts of stars, the energy that powers our lives comes from the Sun, and the space we move through is shaped by the same forces that govern the cosmos.

This chapter is only the beginning. In the chapters to come, we will explore the nature of time and space, the potential for multiple universes, the role of consciousness, and the possibility of life beyond Earth. The universe beckons us to explore its mysteries, to seek out its secrets, and to discover our place within its grand design.

Chapter 1 concludes.

CHAPTER 2
THE DIVINE BLUEPRINT

Chapter 2: The Cosmic Web and Divine Design

The Structure Beneath the Stars

As we peer into the universe, we expect to see stars, galaxies, and planets scattered randomly across the void. But what scientists have uncovered is something far more intricate—a grand, interconnected structure known as the *cosmic web*. This web, made up of invisible dark matter and gas, stretches across the universe, connecting galaxies like pearls on a necklace and creating a design that spans billions of light-years. To understand this vast structure is to gain insight into the forces that shaped the universe itself.

The cosmic web is the universe's hidden skeleton, a delicate yet vast network that connects galaxies and galaxy clusters. It is not just a physical manifestation of the universe's matter but also a symbol of the interconnectedness that binds everything together—both physically and perhaps spiritually. Could this web of galaxies be a reflection of a deeper order, a divine design that we are only beginning to grasp?

Unveiling the Cosmic Web: A Journey Back in Time

The formation of the cosmic web began shortly after the Big Bang. In the universe's infancy, matter was distributed almost evenly, but tiny fluctuations in density, amplified by gravity over billions of years, led to the large-scale structure we see today. Regions with slightly more matter exerted a stronger gravitational pull, drawing in surrounding gas and dark matter. Over time, these regions became the filaments and nodes of the cosmic web, while less dense areas became the vast cosmic voids.

This process can be compared to the way water droplets form on a windowpane. As water gathers, it pulls more water toward it, creating distinct streams and drops. Similarly, as matter coalesced, it formed galaxies and clusters along the filaments of the cosmic web, leaving behind the empty spaces between.

The cosmic web provides a glimpse into the fundamental forces that have shaped the universe since its birth. Gravity plays a central role in pulling matter together, while dark energy, a mysterious force that we will explore later, pushes galaxies apart. The tension between these forces has sculpted the universe into the vast, interconnected structure we see today.

The Role of Dark Matter in the Web

One of the most puzzling aspects of the cosmic web is the role of dark matter—an invisible substance that makes up about 85% of the matter in the universe. While dark matter doesn't emit or absorb light, its gravitational influence is essential in shaping the large-scale structure of the universe. Without dark matter, the cosmic web could not exist.

Dark matter acts as the framework upon which the visible matter, like galaxies, is built. It is the glue that holds galaxies together and the scaffolding that supports the cosmic web. Observations of galaxy rotation curves—how fast stars orbit within galaxies—show that there must be more mass than we can see. This extra mass is dark matter.

To picture this, imagine a spider's web. The web is invisible unless light catches it in just the right way. However, the web's structure is vital for the spider to move across it and capture its prey. Dark matter, like the web, is invisible but crucial for the movement and clustering of galaxies.

Galaxies as Jewels on the Web

If the dark matter filaments are the scaffolding of the cosmic web, then galaxies are like the jewels that adorn it. These glowing clusters of stars and gas are the visible nodes of the web, concentrated at the intersections of the filaments. Galaxies form in the densest regions, where gravity pulls matter together, creating vast clusters and superclusters.

The distribution of galaxies across the web is not random. They follow the pathways laid out by dark matter, forming along the filaments and gathering in clusters where the filaments intersect. These clusters can contain thousands of galaxies, bound together by their mutual gravitational pull. In between the filaments lie the cosmic voids, enormous regions of space with very few galaxies.

The scale of these structures is staggering. The largest known structure in the universe is the Hercules-Corona Borealis Great Wall, a supercluster of galaxies stretching over 10 billion light-years across. It is a part of the cosmic web, a reminder of the vastness of the universe and the intricate design that underlies it.

The Balance of Forces: Gravity and Dark Energy

The cosmic web is shaped by two competing forces: gravity and dark energy. Gravity pulls matter together, forming galaxies, clusters, and filaments, while dark energy pushes the universe apart, driving its expansion. This cosmic tug-of-war has defined the universe's evolution.

Gravity, as we understand it, works over long distances, pulling objects together. It is responsible for the formation of stars, galaxies, and galaxy clusters. Dark energy, on the other hand, is a mysterious force that is causing the expansion of the universe to accelerate. Discovered in the late 1990s, dark energy is still poorly understood, but it makes up about 68% of the universe's total energy content.

The cosmic web is a result of the balance between these forces. In the early universe, gravity dominated, pulling matter together to form the web's filaments. But as the universe expanded, dark energy began to play a larger role, pushing galaxies apart and stretching the web.

This balance is delicate. If dark energy were stronger, the universe might have expanded too quickly for galaxies to form. If gravity were stronger, the universe might have collapsed back in on itself. The cosmic web is a product of these finely tuned forces, a testament to the delicate balance that shapes the universe.

Divine Geometry: The Sacred Patterns of the Cosmos

The cosmic web is not just a physical structure; it is also a reflection of the underlying order of the universe. The intricate patterns of galaxies and voids resemble the fractal patterns we see in nature, from the branching of trees to the formation of rivers. These patterns, known as *self-similarity*, occur when a structure looks the same at different scales.

Fractals are a common feature of the natural world, and they reveal the deep connections between seemingly unrelated phenomena. The same branching patterns that govern the formation of galaxies can be found in the distribution of rivers across a landscape, or in the way blood vessels branch through the human body.

This self-similarity suggests that the universe operates according to a deeper, underlying order. The cosmic web, with its filaments and voids, is not a random arrangement but a manifestation of the mathematical laws that govern the cosmos.

For many, these patterns hint at a divine design—a reflection of the mind of the universe's creator. The cosmic web, like a piece of sacred geometry, reveals the hidden structure of the universe, a structure that is both beautiful and functional.

Interconnectedness: The Web of Life and the Cosmos

The cosmic web's structure can also be seen as a metaphor for the interconnectedness of all things. Just as galaxies are connected by invisible filaments of dark matter, so too are we connected to the universe in ways that are not always visible. We are made of the same elements as the stars, and the forces that shaped the cosmic web also shaped the atoms in our bodies.

This interconnectedness is a theme found in many spiritual traditions. In Hinduism, the concept of *Brahman* represents the ultimate reality, the infinite consciousness that connects all things. In Buddhism, the idea of interdependence teaches that nothing exists in isolation—everything is connected in a web of cause and effect.

The cosmic web is a physical manifestation of this interconnectedness.

It reminds us that we are not isolated beings but part of a vast, interconnected universe. Our lives, like the galaxies in the web, are shaped by invisible forces that bind us together.

The Mystery of the Cosmic Web

While we have made great strides in understanding the cosmic web, many questions remain. What is dark matter? What is dark energy? How did the universe evolve from the smooth, featureless early universe to the complex web of galaxies we see today?

These questions drive modern cosmology, pushing scientists to develop new theories and conduct ever more detailed observations. The cosmic web is a reminder that the universe is still full of mysteries, and that our journey to understand it is far from over.

Conclusion: Weaving the Threads of the Universe

The cosmic web is a testament to the interconnectedness of all things. From the largest galaxy clusters to the smallest particles, the universe is bound together by invisible threads of matter and energy. These threads form a grand design, one that stretches across the cosmos and connects everything in it.

As we continue our journey through the universe, we will explore the deeper implications of the cosmic web's design. What does it reveal about the nature of the universe? And what does it tell us about our place in this vast, interconnected cosmos?

The cosmic web is more than just a physical structure—it is a0 reflection of the universe's underlying order, a reminder that everything is connected in a grand, cosmic dance.

Chapter 2 concludes.

Chapter 3

Chapter 3.
The Cosmic Mind

Chapter 3: Time, Creation, and the Infinite (Continued)

Time and Consciousness: Our Perception of Time

One of the most intriguing aspects of time is how we, as conscious beings, perceive it. Our experience of time is deeply subjective—sometimes it seems to fly by, while other times it drags on. This elasticity in how we perceive time suggests that time is not merely an objective property of the universe but is also intertwined with our awareness and consciousness.

In neuroscience, time perception is tied to the brain's processing of events. The more information we process, the slower time seems to pass. Conversely, in routine or monotonous moments, our brain processes less information, making time seem to move faster. This fluidity in our perception of time raises a profound question: Is time an external entity, or is it something that exists only in the mind?

Some theories propose that our sense of time is a construct of consciousness—without consciousness, time may not exist in the way we experience it. This ties into philosophical questions about the nature of reality: If there were no conscious observers, would time continue to flow, or does consciousness play a fundamental role in shaping time itself?

The End of Time: Cosmic Scenarios and the Ultimate Fate

While the origin of time is often associated with the Big Bang, the eventual fate of time is just as mysterious. There are several theories about how the universe—and thus time—might end:

- **Heat Death**: In this scenario, the universe continues expanding, and over billions of years, it reaches a state of maximum entropy. All stars burn out, galaxies drift apart, and eventually, the universe becomes a cold, dark, and inert place. Time, as we know it, would cease to have any meaning in such a state of maximum disorder.
- **The Big Crunch**: As mentioned earlier, the Big Crunch theory suggests that after expanding for billions of years, the universe may begin contracting due to gravitational forces. In this scenario, time would effectively "reverse" as the universe collapses back into a singularity, possibly leading to another Big Bang and a new cycle of time.
- **The Big Rip**: Another possibility is the Big Rip, where the expansion of the universe accelerates due to dark energy, causing galaxies, stars, and even atoms to be torn apart. In this scenario, the fabric of spacetime itself is ripped apart, and time would come to an abrupt and catastrophic end.
- **The Multiverse**: Some cosmologists propose that our universe is just one of many in a multiverse, with each universe having its own version of time. In this model, while time might end in our universe, it could continue indefinitely in others, suggesting that time is not a universal property but a local phenomenon tied to individual universes.

Each of these scenarios provides a glimpse into the vast, unfathomable future of the cosmos and time itself. Whether time will continue indefinitely or come to a final end remains one of the greatest questions in both science and philosophy.

Time and Free Will: Are We Prisoners of Time?

Time also raises profound questions about free will and determinism. If time is a continuous flow from past to future, does that mean our choices are predetermined by prior events? Or does the future remain open, shaped by our actions and decisions?

Some interpretations of quantum mechanics, like the **Many-Worlds Theory**, suggest that every possible outcome of a decision creates a new branch of reality. In this view, there is no single future—there are countless futures, all of which exist simultaneously. Our experience of time, then, is just one of many possible timelines.

In contrast, the idea of **block time**, or the "block universe" theory, posits that the past, present, and future all coexist in a four-dimensional spacetime block. In this view, time is like a landscape—every moment exists, but we can only experience it sequentially. Free will, in this case, may be an illusion, as the future is already set.

The Infinite Present: The Intersection of Time and Eternity

If time is a river, as the metaphor suggests, what lies beyond the river's edge? Could there be an eternal, timeless reality—a state of being that transcends the flow of time?

In many spiritual traditions, the concept of eternity is not just a prolonged stretch of time but a state of timelessness, where the past, present, and future merge into a single, infinite "now." This eternal present is often seen as the realm of the divine—a space where time, as we understand it, does not exist.

In Christian theology, God is often described as eternal, existing outside the bounds of time. Similarly, in Hinduism and Buddhism, states of spiritual enlightenment, such as **moksha** or **nirvana**, are described as transcending time. These traditions suggest that while we live within time, it is possible to experience moments of timelessness, where we connect with a deeper, eternal reality.

This idea of timelessness also resonates with modern physics. In the theory of **spacetime**, time is simply another dimension, and from a higher-dimensional perspective, all moments might exist simultaneously. From this viewpoint, the flow of time is a feature of our limited perspective, and in reality, time may not flow at all.

Time and the Divine: Creation Beyond Time

As we explore the concept of time, we are inevitably drawn to the mystery of creation itself. If time began with the Big Bang, what existed "before" time? How could the universe be created in the absence of time?

In many religious traditions, God is seen as existing outside of time, as the eternal creator. From this perspective, creation is not an event that happened at a specific moment in time, but rather an ongoing process that exists outside of the temporal flow. The universe, in this view, is a manifestation of a timeless divine will—a creation that transcends the constraints of time and space.

This concept of a timeless creator aligns with the idea of the **multiverse**, where creation is not a singular event but a constant process, with countless universes being born, evolving, and dissolving in an eternal cycle. In this infinite cosmic landscape, time itself may be just one dimension of a much larger, more complex reality.

Conclusion: Time, Creation, and the Infinite

Time is one of the most enigmatic forces in the universe. It shapes the cosmos, governs the course of history, and structures our very perception of reality. Yet despite its omnipresence, time remains elusive, a mystery that we are only beginning to understand.

Whether time is a river, flowing from past to future, or an ocean, where all moments exist simultaneously, its role in the universe is profound. It connects creation to destruction, the finite to the infinite, and the material to the spiritual. As we journey through time, we are not just passive observers—we are active participants in the unfolding of the cosmos, shaping the future with our choices and actions.

As we continue to explore the mysteries of time, we are also drawn toward the infinite, the timeless reality that lies beyond the edges of our understanding. In this intersection between time and eternity, we may glimpse the deeper truths of existence and our place in the grand design of the universe.

Chapter 3 concludes.

Chapter 4: Patterns in the Chaos of Creation

Chaos and the Birth of Order

At first glance, the universe may appear chaotic. Stars explode in supernovae, galaxies collide, and black holes devour matter. On our planet, nature itself can seem unpredictable—storms arise suddenly, rivers carve new paths, and ecosystems fluctuate in ways we don't always anticipate. And yet, beneath this apparent chaos lies a surprising truth: there is order, a hidden structure that governs the cosmos at every level.

Scientists have discovered that chaos is not the opposite of order, but rather its partner in a delicate dance. In fact, much of the structure we see in the universe emerges from chaotic systems. From the formation of galaxies to the branching of trees, patterns arise that repeat themselves across different scales, revealing a deeper underlying order in the cosmos.

In this chapter, we will explore the concept of chaos and order, examining how these two forces interact to create the universe as we know it. Through analogies, scientific insights, and imagination, we will uncover the hidden patterns that govern everything from the motion of planets to the growth of living organisms.

Fractals: Nature's Repeating Patterns

One of the most striking examples of order emerging from chaos is the concept of *fractals*. A fractal is a self-similar pattern, meaning that the same shape or structure repeats at different scales. Fractals are found everywhere in nature, from the branching of trees and rivers to the formation of clouds and galaxies. The beauty of fractals lies in their complexity—no matter how closely you zoom in or out, you'll always find the same pattern repeating.

Take, for example, the branching pattern of a river. At first glance, a river may seem to flow randomly across the landscape, but when viewed from above, a clear structure emerges. The main river branches into smaller streams, and those streams branch into even smaller tributaries, following a fractal pattern. The same is true for the blood vessels in your body or the veins in a leaf—they all follow this same fractal geometry.

Fractals also appear in the large-scale structure of the universe. The cosmic web, which we explored in Chapter 2, follows a fractal-like pattern, with galaxies clustering together in filaments that stretch across space. These filaments branch out into smaller structures, creating a cosmic pattern that mirrors the branching of trees or rivers.

This fractal nature of the universe suggests that the same rules that govern the growth of trees also govern the formation of galaxies. It is as if the universe follows a set of mathematical principles that apply at every scale, from the smallest atom to the largest galaxy cluster.

Chaos Theory: Finding Order in Disorder

Another important concept in understanding the balance between chaos and order is *chaos theory*. Chaos theory explores how small changes in the initial conditions of a system can led to vastly different outcomes. This is often referred to as the "butterfly effect"—the idea that the flap of a butterfly's wings in one part of the world could set off a chain of events that leads to a hurricane on the other side of the planet.

At first glance, chaotic systems seem unpredictable, but chaos theory reveals that there is an underlying order in even the most seemingly random processes. For example, weather patterns, while complex and difficult to predict, follow certain rules that allow us to understand the general principles behind storms, winds, and rainfall.

In the universe, chaos theory plays a crucial role in everything from the orbits of planets to the formation of stars. Consider the early moments of the universe after the Big Bang. Tiny fluctuations in the density of matter, almost imperceptible differences in temperature and pressure, were amplified by gravity over billions of years, leading to the formation of galaxies, stars, and planets. What seemed like chaotic fluctuations in the early universe eventually gave rise to the ordered structures we see today.

This interplay between chaos and order is one of the most profound insights of modern science. It suggests that the universe is not random, but follows a set of rules that allow order to emerge from even the most chaotic systems.

The Universe's Hidden Order: The Role of Mathematics

Underlying the universe's apparent chaos is the language of mathematics. From the motion of planets to the behavior of subatomic particles, the universe operates according to precise mathematical laws. These laws describe everything from the curvature of space-time to the energy levels of atoms.

Mathematics is not just a tool for describing the universe—it is a reflection of the universe's underlying order. The equations of general relativity, for example, describe how gravity shapes the fabric of space and time, while the equations of quantum mechanics the behavior of particles at the smallest scales. Both sets of equations, despite their differences, reveal a universe that operates according to a set of fundamental principles.

But where do these mathematical laws come from? Are they simply a human invention, or do they exist independently of us, waiting to be discovered? Some scientists and philosophers believe that mathematics is a universal language, a code that underlies the fabric of reality itself. Others argue that mathematics is a product of the human mind, a tool we use to make sense of the world.

Regardless of their origin, these mathematical laws are the key to understanding how order emerges from chaos. They allow us to predict the motion of planets, the behavior of particles, and even the evolution of galaxies. Without them, the universe would be incomprehensible.

The Role of Entropy: Order and Disorder in the Universe

At the heart of the relationship between chaos and order is the concept of *entropy*. Entropy is a measure of disorder in a system, and according to the second law of thermodynamics, entropy tends to increase over time. This means that systems naturally move from a state of order to a state of disorder.

But entropy is not just about disorder—it also plays a crucial role in the emergence of order. For example, the formation of stars is a process of increasing entropy. As a cloud of gas collapses under the force of gravity, it becomes more disordered, but at the same time, it gives rise to a highly ordered structure: a star.

This paradoxical relationship between order and disorder is one of the most fascinating aspects of the universe. It suggests that order and chaos are not opposites, but two sides of the same coin. Entropy drives the universe toward disorder, but in doing so, it creates the conditions for new forms of order to emerge.

This interplay between order and disorder is what allows the universe to evolve. Without entropy, the universe would be static and unchanging. But with entropy, the universe is dynamic, constantly changing and giving rise to new forms of complexity.

Self-Organization: The Universe's Natural Tendency

One of the most remarkable properties of chaotic systems is their ability to self-organize. Self-organization is the process by which complex structures arise spontaneously from simple interactions. In the universe, self-organization is responsible for the formation of stars, galaxies, and even life itself.

Take, for example, the formation of a star. A cloud of gas and dust, floating in space, may seem like a chaotic and disordered system. But over time, gravity pulls the gas and dust together, creating a highly ordered structure: a star. This process of self-organization is not directed by any external force—it is a natural consequence of the laws of physics.

The same principle applies to the formation of galaxies. In the early universe, matter was distributed almost evenly, but tiny fluctuations in density allowed some regions to collapse under their own gravity, forming galaxies. Over billions of years, these galaxies merged and grew, creating the vast structures we see today.

Self-organization is also at work in biological systems. Life itself is a product of self-organization, as simple molecules come together to form complex organisms. This process is not directed by any external force, but arises naturally from the interactions between molecules.

This ability of the universe to self-organize suggests that order is not imposed from the outside, but emerges naturally from the laws of physics. It is as if the universe has a built-in tendency toward complexity, a drive to create order from chaos.

Chaos and the Emergence of Life

Life is perhaps the most extraordinary example of order emerging from chaos. The origin of life is one of the great mysteries of science, but what we do know is that life arose from the simple building blocks of matter. Over billions of years, simple molecules combined to form more complex structures, eventually giving rise to living organisms.

The process by which life emerged is a perfect example of chaos leading to order. The early Earth was a chaotic environment, with volcanic activity, lightning storms, and intense radiation. And yet, from this chaos, the first living cells emerged. These cells were simple at first, but over time, they evolved into the complex organisms that populate the Earth today.

The evolution of life is itself a chaotic process. Small mutations in the genetic code can lead to significant changes in an organism's structure and behavior. These changes, while often random, are shaped by natural selection, which favors traits that improve an organism's chances of survival. Over time, this process leads to the emergence of highly ordered and complex systems, such as the human brain.

The Harmony of Chaos and Order: A Cosmic Dance

As we explore the interplay between chaos and order, we begin to see that the universe is not a place of random events, but a harmonious system where chaos and order coexist. The same forces that create turbulence in a river also carve out its path. The same gravitational forces that lead to the collapse of stars also give rise to galaxies.

This harmony is reflected in the patterns we see all around us. From the fractal shapes of trees and rivers to the spirals of galaxies, the universe is full of structures that arise from the dynamic interaction of chaos and order. These patterns suggest that the universe operates according to a set of principles that are both mathematical and creative—a cosmic dance in which randomness and structure are partners, not enemies.

For many, this dance between chaos and order hints at a deeper truth about the nature of the universe. It suggests that creation is not a static event but an ongoing process, a continuous unfolding of complexity and beauty. The universe, far from being a random collection of matter, is a place of deep interconnectedness, where chaos gives birth to order, and order allows new forms of chaos to emerge.

Conclusion: Patterns in the Chaos of Creation

In this chapter, we have explored how order emerges from chaos in the universe. From fractals to self-organization, the cosmos is full of hidden structures that reveal the underlying order of creation. While chaos may seem to be a force of destruction, it is also a force of creation, giving rise to the complex patterns that shape everything from galaxies to living organisms.

The universe, it turns out, is not a random place. It is a carefully balanced system, where chaos and order work together to create the structures, we see around us. Whether through the branching of rivers or the formation of stars, the universe follows a set of principles that allow for the emergence of complexity and beauty.

As we continue our journey through the cosmos, we will delve deeper into these principles, exploring how they shape not only the universe but also our understanding of life, time, and consciousness. The dance between chaos and order is one of the most fundamental forces in the universe, and it offers us a glimpse into the profound interconnectedness of all things.

Chapter 4 concludes.

Chapter 5

Chapter 5: The Microcosm, the Macrocosm, and God's Perspective

The Universe in Every Scale

As we explore the universe, we find that it operates on many different scales—from the smallest particles that make up atoms to the vast structures of galaxies and galaxy clusters that span billions of light-years. This is the mystery of the *microcosm* and the *macrocosm*—the idea that the same patterns and principles that govern the smallest particles also govern the largest structures in the universe. In other words, the universe is self-similar across different scales, with the small and the large reflecting one another.

Consider the structure of an atom, with electrons orbiting a nucleus in much the same way that planets orbit a star. The forces that bind subatomic particles together are analogous to the gravitational forces that hold galaxies in place. And just as galaxies cluster together in vast networks, so too do the particles in our bodies form complex structures, such as cells, organs, and organisms.

This idea of the microcosm and macrocosm raises profound questions about the nature of the universe. Could it be that the same laws of physics that govern the behavior of atoms also shape the structure of galaxies? And if so, what does this tell us about the deeper order of the cosmos? Could the patterns we observe at the smallest scales be a reflection of a greater, divine order that governs the entire universe?

Fractals: The Universe's Repeating Patterns

One of the most striking features of the universe is the presence of *fractals*—self-repeating patterns that occur at different scales. We see these patterns in the branching of trees, the flow of rivers, and the shapes of clouds. Fractals are also present in the large-scale structure of the universe, where galaxies form clusters and filaments that resemble the branching of rivers or the veins in a leaf.

Fractals suggest that the universe is governed by the same principles at all levels of existence. The same forces that shape the structure of a river are at work in the formation of galaxies. This self-similarity hints at a deeper unity between the microcosm and the macrocosm, a connection that ties together the smallest particles with the largest galaxies.

For example, the branching structure of a tree, with its trunk splitting into branches and those branches splitting into smaller branches, follows the same mathematical principles as the way galaxies cluster together in the cosmic web. This repeating pattern across scales is a reflection of the universe's underlying order, an order that seems to govern everything from the behavior of electrons to the motion of stars.

Life as the Bridge Between Scales

Life itself occupies a unique place in this cosmic hierarchy. We are made up of trillions of cells, each one a tiny universe in itself, with molecules and atoms interacting in complex ways. Yet we are also part of the larger universe, living on a planet that orbits a star in a galaxy that is part of the cosmic web.

In this way, life is the bridge between the microcosm and the macrocosm. Through our bodies, we experience the small-scale world of atoms and molecules, but through our minds, we contemplate the vastness of the cosmos. We are both observers of the universe and participants in its unfolding.

Just as galaxies are connected by the cosmic web, the cells in our bodies are connected by networks of communication, allowing us to function as a single, unified organism. The same principles that govern the organization of galaxies also govern the organization of life, suggesting that life is not separate from the universe but an integral part of its structure.

God's Perspective: The Unity of Creation

If the universe is self-similar across different scales, then from the perspective of a higher power, the distinction between the small and the large may not exist. To a being that exists outside of time and space, the smallest atom and the largest galaxy may be equally significant—both part of the same grand design.

This idea is reflected in many spiritual traditions. In Hinduism, for example, the divine is seen as present in all things, from the smallest particles to the largest structures. In Christianity, God is described as omnipresent, meaning that God is present everywhere, in every part of creation.

The concept of God as the creator of both the microcosm and the macrocosm suggests that the universe is not a collection of separate parts but a unified whole. Every particle, every star, every living being is part of the same divine plan, a reflection of the same underlying reality.

The Cosmic Web and the Web of Life

Just as the cosmic web connects galaxies across the universe, the web of life connects all living beings on Earth. From the smallest microorganisms to the largest mammals, life is interconnected in a delicate balance of ecosystems and habitats. The food we eat, the air we breathe, and the water we drink are all part of this intricate web, and our actions ripple through it in ways we may not fully understand.

This interconnectedness is a reflection of the larger cosmic order. Just as galaxies are not isolated entities but part of a larger structure, so too are we connected to the world around us. Our lives are shaped by the same forces that shape the universe, and our actions have consequences that extend far beyond our individual selves.

This idea of interconnectedness is central to many spiritual traditions. In Buddhism, for example, the concept of interdependence teaches that all things are connected in a web of cause and effect. In Hinduism, the idea of *Brahman* represents the ultimate reality that connects all beings and all things.

The cosmic web and the web of life remind us that we are not separate from the universe but part of a grand design that spans both the smallest particles and the largest galaxies.

The Mystery of the Microcosm and the Macrocosm

Despite our understanding of the universe, many mysteries remain.

How is it that the same principles that govern the behavior of atoms also govern the formation of galaxies?

What connects the microcosm and the macrocosm? These questions touch on some of the deepest mysteries of existence and hint at a reality that is far more complex than we can imagine.

One possibility is that the universe is not just a physical structure but also a manifestation of a deeper, metaphysical order. In this view, the patterns we see in the universe are not just the result of physical forces but reflections of a deeper, spiritual reality.

The microcosm and the macrocosm are not separate realms but two sides of the same coin, both part of the same divine order.

This idea is echoed in the ancient concept of the *Great Chain of Being*, which suggests that all things in the universe are connected in a hierarchical order, from the smallest particles to the highest forms of consciousness. In this view, the universe is a reflection of a higher, spiritual reality, with each level of existence connected to the next.

Conclusion: The Unity of Creation

As we contemplate the relationship between the microcosm and the macrocosm, we begin to see that the universe is a unified whole, governed by the same principles at every level. The patterns we observe in nature, from the branching of trees to the structure of galaxies, are reflections of the same underlying order, an order that ties together the entire cosmos.

In this unity, we find a profound connection between the small and the large, the individual and the universe. And in this connection, we glimpse the possibility that all of creation is part of a single, divine web—one that stretches across all scales, from the smallest atom to the largest galaxy.

As we continue our journey through the cosmos, we will explore the deeper implications of this unity and what it means for our understanding of life, consciousness, and the nature of reality.

Chapter 5 concludes.

Chapter 5A

Chapter 5A

Chapter 5A: The Glass of Mud Water and the Infinite Scale of Existence

A Simple Glass: A World Hidden in Plain Sight

At first glance, a simple glass of murky water scooped from a muddy pond may seem like a humble, uneventful object. The water is unclear, tainted by floating particles, and it may appear disordered, unattractive, or even uninteresting. However, if we peer closer, aided by a microscope, we are thrust into a hidden reality, one where the chaotic appearance of the water transforms into a bustling universe.

Inside this small glass of mud water, microorganisms swim with purpose, particles of matter interact in subtle but profound ways, and invisible forces shape the micro-world. Bacteria, algae, and protozoa—all existing in quantities too vast to imagine—compete, cooperate, and coexist, living out their life cycles in a world we could easily dismiss.

This analogy holds powerful insight into the nature of the universe at large. If we can overlook the hidden complexity in something as simple as a glass of water, could it be that we are missing similar layers of reality in the cosmos? Perhaps, to a higher power—one that exists beyond time and space—our entire universe, with its seemingly endless galaxies and grand structures, is no more significant than a glass of mud water.

As we examine the layers of complexity within that small glass, it invites us to consider: What lies beyond the boundaries of our perception? Just as a microscope reveals hidden depths in water, are there tools or perspectives that could help us uncover the deeper truths of the universe? What if our universe is just one among many, existing within a grander framework of reality, each layer more intricate than the last?

Peering Downward: The Invisible Depths Below Microbes

The glass of mud water offers us a portal into the world of microbes. The smallest forms of life—bacteria, single-celled organisms, and viruses—exist in vast numbers, each playing a critical role in the ecosystems they inhabit. These organisms may be invisible to the naked eye, but their impact on the world is undeniable.

Yet, as we journey deeper, we discover that even microbes are composed of smaller building blocks. Beneath the microbial level lies the molecular world. Molecules, consisting of atoms bound together by electromagnetic forces, serve as the foundation of all biological processes. Proteins, in particular, are molecular machines that perform critical functions in every living cell.

DNA, the molecule that encodes the instructions for life, twists and coils into a double-helix, storing vast amounts of information within its chemical structure. Every organism, from the smallest bacterium to the largest mammal, depends on DNA for its growth, development, and survival. But even DNA is not the final frontier of smallness. Beneath the molecular scale lies the atomic realm, where individual atoms—tiny, invisible to even the most powerful microscopes—serve as the fundamental building blocks of matter.

Each atom, in turn, is composed of subatomic particles: protons, neutrons, and electrons. These particles form the heart of every atom, held together by forces that operate on scales beyond our everyday experience. But even here, the journey is far from over. Inside protons and neutrons are even smaller particles known as quarks, which combine in different configurations to give rise to the familiar particles of the atomic nucleus.

At these subatomic levels, the rules of classical physics begin to break down, and we enter the strange world of quantum mechanics. In this world, particles do not behave in predictable ways. Instead, they exist in states of probability, where they can occupy multiple positions or states simultaneously. This world defies the logic of our everyday experiences, suggesting that reality is far more complex and mysterious than we often assume.

Could there be yet more levels beyond the quantum? Some physicists theorize the existence of strings, one-dimensional objects that vibrate at different frequencies to give rise to particles as we know them. If this theory, known as string theory, is correct, then we are just beginning to scratch the surface of the true nature of matter.

The Microscopic Reality: Life at Tiny Scales

Though we think of ourselves as beings at the centre of reality, our existence is built upon the labour of countless invisible processes. Every second, millions of cells in our bodies divide, heal, and regenerate. We exist as a collection of living cells, each containing the same complex machinery found in the glass of mud water.

Inside each cell, organelles—tiny structures—perform specific tasks, much like organs in a human body. The mitochondria generate energy, the ribosomes build proteins, and the nucleus serves as the control centre, directing the cell's activity through the genetic information contained in DNA.

These processes are not unique to humans. Every organism on Earth, from the simplest bacteria to the most complex animals, depends on this microscopic reality. Yet, despite their importance, we rarely stop to consider the fact that our existence is supported by systems so small that they operate below our perception.

The deeper we look into this microscopic world, the more we find that there is no clear boundary between life and non-life. Viruses, for example, occupy a strange space between the living and the non-living. They cannot replicate on their own but hijack the machinery of living cells to reproduce.

The Scale Beyond the Stars: Expanding the Universe Outward

From the tiny, hidden world of microbes, molecules, and atoms, we shift our focus outward. The Earth, our home, is one of countless planets that orbit the Sun, which in turn is one star among billions in the Milky Way galaxy. The Milky Way itself is just one of trillions of galaxies scattered throughout the observable universe. Each galaxy contains billions of stars, planets, and potentially countless forms of life.

At these cosmic scales, distances become almost impossible to grasp. Light, which travels at 299,792 kilometres per second, takes more than four years to reach us from our nearest star, Proxima Centauri. The distance between galaxies is measured in millions of light-years, vast stretches of emptiness separating the luminous islands of matter.

As we zoom out further, we encounter galaxy clusters and superclusters, vast collections of galaxies bound together by gravity. These structures stretch across hundreds of millions of light-years, forming the backbone of the universe's large-scale structure. And beyond even these superclusters lie the cosmic web.

The cosmic web is the large-scale structure of the universe, a network of galaxies connected by filaments of dark matter and gas. These filaments stretch across the universe, linking galaxy clusters in a web-like pattern that resembles the neural pathways of the human brain. Just as cells in our bodies are interconnected by networks of communication, so too are galaxies connected by the cosmic web.

The Concept of the Multiverse: A Universe Among Many

As we continue to expand outward, we begin to wonder: is there a limit to the universe? Could it be that our universe is just one among many, each existing in a larger multiverse? The idea of the multiverse suggests that beyond our observable universe, there may be countless other universes, each with its own laws of physics and its own unique structures.

Some scientists believe that these universes may have formed during the early moments of the Big Bang when space itself was expanding at an exponential rate. Others propose that universes are constantly being born and dying in a never-ending cycle of creation and destruction.

The multiverse theory raises profound questions about the nature of reality. If there are infinite universes, each with its own possibilities, then anything that can happen does happen somewhere. Every decision, every action, may create a new branch of reality, a new universe where events unfold in different ways.

Time and Scale: An Expanding Concept of Reality

Just as space expands outward to unimaginable distances, so too does time stretch across scales that are difficult for us to comprehend. For a bacterium, time flows rapidly—its entire life cycle may unfold in a matter of hours. For a star, time moves slowly, with billions of years passing between its birth and eventual death.

The perception of time shifts depending on the scale at which we observe it. For us, a human lifetime may seem long, but to a galaxy, it is the blink of an eye. Likewise, for a microbe, a second may seem like an eternity.

This scaling of time invites us to consider how time might be perceived by other forms of life, or even by the universe itself. If we are capable of experiencing time in such a limited way, what might it be like for a higher power to perceive time across the entire span of the universe? Could time itself be an illusion, a construct of our limited understanding?

The Divine Perspective: A Higher Understanding

If there exists a being beyond time and space—a higher power—then the distinction between the microcosm and the macrocosm may dissolve entirely. To such a being, the smallest particle and the largest galaxy may appear as part of the same unified whole. The glass of mud water, teeming with life, and the vast cosmic web, stretching across billions of light-years, may be equally significant.

This idea of divine unity is reflected in many spiritual traditions. In Hinduism, the concept of Brahman represents the ultimate reality, the Brahman represents the ultimate reality, the universal spirit that underlies and connects all beings and things. In this view, every particle of existence, whether it is a quark in the quantum world or a star in a distant galaxy, is part of a single, indivisible whole. Similarly, in Christianity, the concept of God's omnipresence reflects the belief that the divine is present everywhere, from the smallest atom to the farthest reaches of the cosmos.

In such spiritual perspectives, the universe is not a collection of isolated parts, but a harmonious, interconnected system where every component, no matter how small or large, plays a role in the grand design. The glass of mud water, then, becomes a powerful metaphor for the way the divine sees the world—every element, every being, and every particle is significant in the larger scheme of creation. Just as we might observe the intricacies within that glass, a higher power might observe the unfolding of the universe, seeing the harmony between the microcosm and the macrocosm.

The Infinite Layers of Reality: From Quarks to the Cosmos

If we follow the trail of this analogy further, we begin to imagine a universe built upon infinite layers of reality. Just as the world of the microbe gives way to molecules, atoms, and quarks, and just as the world of galaxies expands into clusters, superclusters, and cosmic webs, there may be no end to the scales of existence. Could the universe extend endlessly downward into smaller and smaller particles, just as it expands outward into larger and larger structures?

This concept of infinite scales suggests that the universe may be self-similar at every level. The same patterns and principles that govern the behaviour of galaxies might also govern the behaviour of atoms. This idea is reflected in fractal geometry, where patterns repeat at different scales, from the smallest to the largest.

In a fractal universe, there would be no final "building block" of reality—each level would reveal new complexities, new structures, and new possibilities.

Every atom, every molecule, and every galaxy might contain within it the seeds of an even greater reality, just as the glass of mud water contains entire worlds within it. This infinite progression challenges our understanding of the universe and invites us to consider that the journey of discovery may never truly end.

This leads to a profound realization: we may never fully grasp the true nature of the universe, but that does not diminish the beauty of the quest. The more we explore, the more we uncover the interconnectedness of all things. The universe, like the glass of mud water, is filled with hidden wonders waiting to be revealed, each discovery opening the door to even deeper mysteries.

The Web That Binds All Things: Interconnectedness at Every Scale

One of the most striking revelations of modern science is the interconnectedness of all things. Whether we are examining the behaviour of subatomic particles or studying the motion of galaxies, we find that nothing exists in isolation. The universe operates as a vast, interconnected web, where every action has consequences that ripple through space and time.

This web of interconnectedness can be seen in both the physical world and the biological world. In physics, the phenomenon of quantum entanglement shows that particles can be connected in such a way that the state of one particle instantly affects the state of another, even if they are separated by vast distances. This suggests that the universe is deeply interconnected at the quantum level, with information traveling faster than the speed of light.

In the biological world, we see this interconnectedness in the web of life. Every organism, no matter how small, plays a role in the larger ecosystem. Plants, animals, bacteria, and fungi all interact in a delicate balance, sustaining the cycles of life.

This interconnectedness is essential to the survival of life on Earth, just as the cosmic web binds galaxies together in the universe.

The glass of mud water serves as a metaphor for this universal web. Just as the particles and organisms in the water interact in complex ways, shaping the environment within the glass, so too do the stars, planets, and galaxies shape the structure of the universe. From the smallest scales to the largest, the universe is a dynamic system, where every part is connected to every other part.

Humanity's Place in the Infinite Web

As we contemplate the infinite scales of existence, we must also consider our own place in the universe. Are we insignificant, tiny beings in a vast cosmos, or are we an integral part of a grander design? The answer, perhaps, is both.

On the one hand, humanity is small. We inhabit a small planet orbiting an average star in an unremarkable galaxy, in a universe that may contain billions of galaxies.

From this perspective, our lives may seem fleeting and insignificant. And yet, the very fact that we can contemplate the universe, that we can peer into the glass of mud water and understand the complexity it contains, suggests that we play a unique role in the cosmic web.

Through science, art, philosophy, and spirituality, we seek to understand the mysteries of the universe. Our quest for knowledge is a reflection of the universe's own complexity, and our desire to explore the unknown is a testament to our deep connection with the cosmos. In this sense, humanity is both a participant and an observer in the unfolding of the universe.

Conclusion: The Infinite Mystery of the Universe

The glass of mud water serves as a powerful symbol of the infinite mystery of the universe. What seems simple and chaotic on the surface reveals deeper levels of complexity when viewed through the right lens.

Whether we are looking at the smallest particles of matter or the largest structures in the cosmos, we find that the universe is a web of interconnected systems, each contributing to the whole.

As we continue our journey of discovery, we are reminded that the universe may be infinite—not just in size, but in complexity. Every layer we uncover reveals new worlds, new patterns, and new possibilities.

The deeper we look, the more we realize how little we truly know. But this ignorance is not a weakness; it is the source of our curiosity, our wonder, and our desire to explore. Just as the glass of mud water contains hidden worlds, so too does the universe contain layers of reality that we are only beginning to understand.

The quest for knowledge is an endless journey, one that will take us from the smallest scales of existence to the farthest reaches of the cosmos. And along the way, we will discover that we are part of something far greater than ourselves.

In the end, the universe, like the glass of mud water, is both simple and infinitely complex. It is a reflection of the divine, a testament to the interconnectedness of all things, and a reminder that the journey of discovery is one of the greatest adventures of all.

Chapter 5A concludes.

CHAPTER 6
CHAPTER 6

Chapter 6: The Limits of Perception in a Divine Universe

Seeing Only a Fraction of Reality

Our senses are extraordinary, allowing us to navigate the world around us, but they are also incredibly limited. When we look at the night sky, we see only a small fraction of the electromagnetic spectrum—the visible light that our eyes can detect. Beyond that, the universe is filled with invisible phenomena: ultraviolet and infrared light, X-rays, radio waves, and more. The reality we perceive is just a sliver of what truly exists.

Even with advanced technology, such as telescopes and satellites, we can only observe a limited portion of the cosmos. The universe is vast and teeming with forces and particles that lie beyond our direct perception. Dark matter, for example, makes up about 85% of the universe's mass, yet it is completely invisible to us. We know it exists because of its gravitational effects on galaxies, but we cannot see, touch, or directly detect it.

In this chapter, we will explore the limitations of human perception, the invisible forces that shape the universe, and how these limitations might influence our understanding of the divine. What if there are entire dimensions or realms of existence that we cannot perceive? Could these hidden realities be where the divine resides, influencing the universe in ways we are only beginning to grasp?

The Invisible Forces of the Universe

One of the most profound discoveries in modern cosmology is the existence of *dark matter* and *dark energy*, which together make up about 95% of the universe. These forces are invisible, undetectable by traditional means, yet they have a profound impact on the structure and behavior of the cosmos.

Dark Matter:

We cannot see dark matter directly, but we know it exists because of its gravitational effects on visible matter. Without dark matter, galaxies would not hold together; they would fly apart under the influence of their own rotation. Dark matter is like an invisible skeleton, holding the universe together, yet it eludes all attempts to observe it directly.

The discovery of dark matter raises deep questions about the nature of the universe. What is this invisible substance, and how does it interact with the forces we can observe? Could dark matter be part of a hidden realm, one that exists parallel to our own but is beyond our ability to perceive?

Dark Energy:

Even more mysterious than dark matter is dark energy, a force that is driving the accelerated expansion of the universe. Discovered in the late 1990s, dark energy is thought to make up about 68% of the universe's total energy content. It is the reason why galaxies are moving away from each other at an ever-increasing rate.

Dark energy is unlike any force we have ever encountered. It does not interact with matter in the same way that gravity or electromagnetism does, and its nature remains one of the greatest unsolved mysteries in physics. Could dark energy be a manifestation of a deeper, unseen force—a force that operates in dimensions beyond our understanding?

A Higher Perspective: Perceiving Beyond Human Limits

Imagine for a moment that you could perceive the universe not just through your limited human senses but through the eyes of a higher being. A being that is not constrained by the electromagnetic spectrum or the physical laws that bind us. This being would be able to see the entire range of light, from the longest radio waves to the shortest gamma rays. It would perceive the gravitational effects of dark matter as easily as we see sunlight. It might even be able to detect the presence of dark energy, sensing the expansion of the universe like the movement of a breeze.

From this higher perspective, the universe would appear very different from how we see it. Galaxies and stars would be only one small part of the picture. The unseen forces and dimensions that shape the cosmos would be visible, revealing a deeper, more complex reality.

Many spiritual traditions teach that such a perspective is not only possible but is the way the divine views the universe. In Hinduism, the concept of *Brahman* represents the ultimate reality, a consciousness that transcends time, space, and the limitations of human perception. In Christianity, God is often described as omnipresent and omniscient, perceiving all things in their totality, beyond the confines of time and space.

The Veil of Illusion: Maya and the Limits of Perception

In Hindu and Buddhist philosophy, there is a concept known as *maya*, which refers to the illusion that clouds our perception of reality. According to this view, the world we perceive with our senses is not the ultimate reality but a kind of illusion, a limited version of the true nature of the universe.

The idea of *maya* suggests that our senses deceive us, showing us only the surface of things while hiding the deeper, more profound reality. This aligns with modern science's understanding that we see only a fraction of what exists. The visible world is but a thin layer over a much vaster, unseen universe.

In this context, spiritual enlightenment is often described as the lifting of the veil of *maya*. It is the moment when one perceives the true nature of reality, beyond the limitations of human senses. Could it be that the divine, in whatever form one believes, exists in this hidden realm—beyond the veil of *maya*, beyond our limited perception?

Higher Dimensions: The Hidden Realms of Existence

Physicists have long speculated that there may be more dimensions of space beyond the three that we experience in everyday life. In string theory, for example, the universe is thought to have at least ten dimensions, most of which are hidden from our perception. These extra dimensions might be compactified—curled up in such a way that they are undetectable at human scales.

If these higher dimensions exist, they could provide a home for the unseen forces of dark matter and dark energy. They might also offer a realm where the divine resides, influencing the universe in ways that we cannot directly observe.

The idea of higher dimensions is not only a scientific theory; it has been a part of spiritual traditions for millennia. In many belief systems, the divine is said to exist in a higher plane of reality, one that is beyond the reach of human senses. In this view, our perception of the universe is limited to the physical realm, while the true nature of existence lies in a higher dimension—a realm of spirit, consciousness, or energy.

The Search for Meaning Beyond Perception

Our limited perception of the universe forces us to confront some of the deepest questions of existence. What lies beyond what we can see, hear, and touch? How much of reality is hidden from us, just out of reach?

This search for meaning has been at the heart of both science and spirituality for centuries. While science seeks to understand the universe through observation and experimentation, spirituality seeks to understand the deeper, hidden truths that lie beyond our perception.

Many spiritual traditions teach that the material world is only a small part of reality. In Christianity, the concept of heaven suggests that there is a higher realm beyond the physical world, a place of divine presence and eternal life. In Hinduism and Buddhism, the physical world is seen as *samsara*—a cycle of birth, death, and rebirth from which one must escape to reach enlightenment and perceive the true nature of reality.

Both science and spirituality offer us tools to explore the universe, but they also remind us that there are limits to what we can know. The universe is full of mysteries, and much of it remains hidden from view, waiting to be discovered.

The Role of Technology: Expanding Our Perception

While our natural senses are limited, technology has allowed us to extend our perception far beyond what we could achieve on our own. Telescopes allow us to see distant galaxies, microscopes reveal the hidden world of cells and molecules, and particle accelerators probe the fundamental particles that make up the universe.

However, even with the most advanced technology, we are still only scratching the surface. There are regions of space that are forever beyond our reach, hidden by the vast distances of the universe. There are particles and forces that we cannot yet detect, even with the most sensitive instruments.

This limitation reminds us that the universe is far larger and more complex than we can comprehend. Technology may expand our view, but it also shows us the vastness of what we do not know.

Embracing the Mystery of the Unseen

As we contemplate the limits of our perception, we are reminded that the universe is filled with mysteries beyond our understanding. Our senses, while powerful, can only reveal a fraction of reality. Beyond the visible world lies a universe of hidden forces, unseen dimensions, and unknown phenomena.

But rather than seeing these limitations as a barrier, we can embrace them as an invitation to explore, to wonder, and to seek deeper understanding. The unseen universe is not a place of fear or uncertainty, but a realm of infinite possibility, where the mysteries of creation unfold in ways that we have yet to discover.

Conclusion: Expanding Our Vision of the Universe

In this chapter, we have explored the limits of human perception and the invisible forces that shape the universe. From dark matter and dark energy to higher dimensions and spiritual realms, the universe is far more complex than we can perceive with our senses. But these limitations do not diminish the beauty and wonder of the cosmos—they enhance it, reminding us that there is always more to explore.

As we continue our journey through the universe, we will seek to expand our vision, both scientifically and spiritually. The universe invites us to look beyond what we can see and to contemplate the vast, unseen realms that lie just beyond our reach. In doing so, we may find not only a deeper understanding of the cosmos but also a greater connection to the divine.

Chapter 6 concludes.

Chapter 7: God as the Architect of the Cosmos

The Universe: A Grand Design

When we look at the universe, we are often struck by its immense beauty and complexity. From the spiral arms of galaxies to the delicate structure of snowflakes, the universe seems to follow a grand architectural design. This sense of order has led many to wonder: Could the universe be the work of an architect—a divine creator who carefully crafted the cosmos with intention and purpose?

In this chapter, we will explore the idea of God as the architect of the universe, examining how the structure of the cosmos reflects deeper spiritual truths. Whether viewed through the lens of science or spirituality, the universe reveals a remarkable degree of order and precision, suggesting that it is not merely the product of random chance but of a deliberate, intelligent design.

Mathematics: The Language of Creation

One of the most compelling arguments for the idea of a divine architect is the presence of *mathematical order* in the universe. From the orbits of planets to the behavior of subatomic particles, the cosmos appears to be governed by precise mathematical principles. These laws are not arbitrary—they are consistent, predictable, and elegant, often revealing a deep underlying simplicity in even the most complex systems.

For example, the motion of planets around the sun follows Kepler's laws of planetary motion, which describe the precise elliptical orbits that planets trace as they move through space. The force of gravity, as described by Newton's laws, dictates how objects interact with one another, from the smallest particles to the largest galaxies. These laws are mathematical in nature, suggesting that the universe itself operates according to a set of rules that can be expressed in numbers and equations.

Mathematics seems to be the universal language of creation. It is a code that underlies the fabric of reality, governing everything from the formation of galaxies to the structure of DNA. Many scientists and philosophers have argued that the mathematical nature of the universe points to the existence of a divine creator—an architect who designed the cosmos with precision and intention.

Fine-Tuning: A Universe Built for Life

Another aspect of the universe that suggests the hand of a divine architect is the concept of *fine-tuning*. The physical constants of the universe—the values of fundamental forces and particles—are set in such a way that they allow for the existence of life. If any of these constants were even slightly different, the universe would be radically different, and life as we know it would be impossible.

For example, the strength of the gravitational force is finely tuned. If it were slightly stronger, stars would burn through their fuel too quickly, preventing the formation of planets and life. If it were slightly weaker, stars would not ignite, and the universe would be a cold, dark place. The same is true for other forces, such as the electromagnetic force and the strong nuclear force. The values of these forces are just right to allow for the existence of stars, planets, and ultimately life.

This fine-tuning has led many to speculate that the universe was designed with life in mind. Could it be that the physical constants of the universe were set by a divine architect, who carefully adjusted the parameters to ensure that life could emerge? The fine-tuning of the universe suggests that the cosmos is not a random accident but a purposeful creation, designed with a specific goal in mind.

The Geometry of Creation: Sacred Patterns in the Cosmos

The idea of a divine architect is not just a modern concept; it has ancient roots. Many cultures throughout history have viewed the universe as a sacred structure, governed by geometric patterns that reflect the underlying order of creation. The ancient Greeks, for example, believed that the universe was built according to mathematical principles, with geometry playing a central role in the design of the cosmos.

One of the most famous examples of this idea is the *Golden Ratio*, a mathematical ratio that appears in many natural phenomena, from the spirals of galaxies to the shapes of seashells. The Golden Ratio is often associated with beauty and harmony, and it has been used in art and architecture for centuries. Many believe that the presence of the Golden Ratio in nature is evidence of a deeper, divine order—an indication that the universe was designed with intention and care.

Other geometric patterns, such as the Fibonacci sequence and fractals, also appear throughout nature. These patterns are self-replicating and can be found in everything from the branching of trees to the structure of the human body. The recurrence of these patterns suggests that the universe operates according to a set of geometric principles, further reinforcing the idea of a grand design.

Chaos and Order: The Balance of Creation

While the universe exhibits remarkable order, it is also a place of chaos and unpredictability. Stars explode in violent supernovae, black holes devour matter, and galaxies collide in cosmic cataclysms. How can we reconcile this chaos with the idea of a divine architect?

The answer lies in the balance between chaos and order. Just as an architect must balance creativity with structure, the universe seems to be a balance of chaotic forces and underlying order. This balance is what allows the universe to evolve and grow, creating new forms of complexity and beauty.

In chaos theory, we learn that even seemingly random events follow certain rules. The patterns we see in nature, such as the fractal shapes of clouds and rivers, emerge from the interplay between chaos and order. This suggests that chaos is not the opposite of order but a necessary part of creation—a tool that the divine architect uses to shape the universe.

God's Blueprint: The Divine Plan of Creation

If the universe is the work of a divine architect, then it follows that there must be a blueprint—a plan that governs the unfolding of creation. This idea is central to many spiritual traditions, which teach that the universe operates according to a divine plan, one that is beyond human understanding but is nevertheless present in every aspect of creation.

In Christianity, the concept of God's plan is often described as *Providence*—the idea that God is guiding the universe toward a specific goal. In Hinduism, the universe is seen as a manifestation of *Brahman*, the ultimate reality that pervades all things. In both traditions, the universe is viewed as a purposeful creation, with every event and every life having a place in the grand design.

The idea of a divine blueprint is also reflected in the scientific study of the universe. The laws of physics, the fine-tuning of the physical constants, and the geometric patterns that appear throughout nature all suggest that the universe is not a random collection of matter but a carefully crafted design. Whether we view this blueprint as a product of a divine creator or as an inherent feature of the universe, it points to a deeper order that underlies all of creation.

The Role of Consciousness in Creation

If God is the architect of the universe, then what is our role in this grand design? Many spiritual traditions teach that human beings are not passive observers of the universe but active participants in creation. Our consciousness, our ability to think, feel, and create, is seen as a reflection of the divine consciousness that brought the universe into being.

In this view, consciousness is not just a by-product of evolution but a fundamental part of the universe. Just as the architect designs a building with the intention that it will be inhabited, the universe was designed with the intention that conscious beings would emerge to observe and participate in creation.

This idea is supported by modern physics, which suggests that consciousness may play a fundamental role in the nature of reality. In quantum mechanics, for example, the act of observation is said to influence the outcome of experiments, suggesting that consciousness is intimately connected to the fabric of the universe. This idea aligns with the spiritual belief that we are co-creators with the divine, helping to shape the unfolding of the universe through our thoughts and actions.

The Divine Architect and the Future of Creation

If the universe is the work of a divine architect, then what does the future hold? Will the universe continue to evolve, or will it eventually come to an end? These questions have puzzled scientists and theologians alike, but they also offer an opportunity for reflection on the nature of creation.

Many spiritual traditions teach that creation is an ongoing process, one that is constantly evolving and expanding. In Hinduism, the universe goes through cycles of creation and destruction, with each cycle giving rise to new forms of life and consciousness. In Christianity, the concept of the *Kingdom of God* suggests that the universe is moving toward a state of greater harmony and unity.

In science, the future of the universe is uncertain. The universe is currently expanding, but it is unclear whether this expansion will continue indefinitely or if the universe will eventually collapse back in on itself. Regardless of the outcome, the idea of a divine architect suggests that the universe has a purpose, one that transcends the physical limitations of time and space.

Conclusion: The Universe as a Sacred Design

As we contemplate the idea of God as the architect of the universe, we are reminded of the remarkable order and beauty that pervades creation. From the fine-tuning of the physical constants to the geometric patterns that appear throughout nature, the universe seems to follow a grand design, one that reflects the hand of a divine creator.

Whether viewed through the lens of science or spirituality, the universe reveals a deep underlying order, suggesting that it is not a random accident but a purposeful creation. As we continue our journey through the cosmos, we will explore the deeper implications of this design and what it means for our understanding of life, consciousness, and the nature of the divine.

Chapter 7 concludes.

CHAPTER 8

CHAPTER 8

Chapter 8: The Intersection of Science and Spirituality

A Shared Quest for Truth

For centuries, humanity has sought to understand the mysteries of the universe through two seemingly different paths: science and spirituality. Science seeks to explain the physical world through observation, experimentation, and reason, while spirituality seeks to explore the deeper meaning behind existence through faith, intuition, and contemplation. These two approaches are often seen as opposing forces, but in reality, they share a common goal: the search for truth.

In this chapter, we will explore the intersection of science and spirituality, examining how they complement one another in the quest for understanding the universe. While science reveals the mechanics of the cosmos—its laws, forces, and particles—spirituality offers insight into the purpose and meaning behind creation. Together, these two perspectives provide a more complete view of the universe, one that embraces both the material and the metaphysical.

The Big Bang and Creation Myths: Different Stories, Same Truth

One of the most profound areas of convergence between science and spirituality is the question of origins. Science tells us that the universe began roughly 13.8 billion years ago in a massive explosion known as the *Big Bang*. In an instant, all matter, energy, and space-time were created, setting the stage for the evolution of galaxies, stars, planets, and life.

But long before the Big Bang theory was formulated, ancient cultures developed their own explanations for the origins of the universe. Creation myths from various traditions tell of the universe emerging from chaos, from a void, or from the mind of a creator. In Hinduism, for example, the universe is said to have emerged from the cosmic waters, with the god Brahma creating the world through his divine thought. In the Judeo-Christian tradition, God is described as creating the heavens and the earth in six days, bringing order to the formless void.

While the language and imagery of these creation stories differ from the scientific explanation, they share a common theme: the universe had a beginning, and its existence is the result of a profound, creative force. Both science and spirituality seek to explain how the universe came to be, offering different perspectives on the same fundamental question: Why is there something rather than nothing?

Quantum Mechanics and Mysticism: The Nature of Reality

Another area where science and spirituality intersect is in the study of *quantum mechanics*. At the quantum level, the behavior of particles is strange and counterintuitive. Particles can exist in multiple states at once, become entangled across vast distances, and behave unpredictably in ways that defy our everyday understanding of reality.

These strange phenomena have led many scientists and philosophers to draw parallels between quantum physics and ancient mystical traditions. In both science and spirituality, there is a recognition that reality is not fixed but fluid, that the material world is not the ultimate truth, and that our perception of reality may be limited.

For example, in Hinduism and Buddhism, the concept of *maya* suggests that the physical world is an illusion—a veil that obscures the deeper, underlying reality. Similarly, quantum mechanics suggests that the world we observe is only one layer of a much more complex reality, one that operates according to principles we are only beginning to understand.

The intersection of quantum mechanics and mysticism invites us to question the nature of reality itself. Is the world we experience through our senses the true nature of existence, or is it merely a shadow of a deeper, more profound reality?

Consciousness: The Bridge Between Science and Spirit

One of the most intriguing areas of convergence between science and spirituality is the study of *consciousness*. While science seeks to understand the biological and neurological processes that give rise to consciousness, spirituality explores the nature of consciousness as a fundamental aspect of existence.

In many spiritual traditions, consciousness is seen as the essence of the self—the *atman* in Hinduism or the *soul* in Christianity. It is the part of us that transcends the physical body, that connects us to the divine, and that persists beyond death. In science, consciousness is often viewed as a product of the brain, arising from the complex interactions of neurons and electrical signals.

But recent discoveries in neuroscience and quantum physics suggest that consciousness may be more than just a by-product of the brain. Some scientists propose that consciousness could be a fundamental aspect of the universe, much like space, time, and matter. This idea, known as *panpsychism*, suggests that consciousness is present in all things, from the smallest particles to the largest galaxies.

If consciousness is indeed a fundamental part of the universe, then it may serve as the bridge between science and spirituality. Through consciousness, we can explore both the material world and the deeper, metaphysical truths that lie beyond it. Consciousness allows us to perceive the universe, to ask   about its nature, and to seek meaning and purpose in our existence.

The Role of Intuition and Reason in Understanding

Both science and spirituality rely on different methods of understanding. Science emphasizes *reason*—the use of logic, experimentation, and observation to uncover the truths of the universe. Through reason, scientists have been able to discover the laws of physics, the properties of matter, and the forces that govern the cosmos.

Spirituality, on the other hand, emphasizes *intuition*—the deep, inner knowing that comes from meditation, contemplation, and spiritual experience. Intuition allows individuals to connect with the divine, to understand the nature of existence on a personal, emotional, and spiritual level.

While reason and intuition are often seen as opposing forces, they are actually complementary. Science and spirituality each offer different tools for understanding the universe, and both are necessary for a complete understanding of reality. Reason allows us to explore the physical world, while intuition helps us to explore the metaphysical. Together, they provide a more holistic view of existence.

The Spiritual Implications of Scientific Discoveries

Scientific discoveries often have profound spiritual implications, forcing us to rethink our place in the universe and our relationship with the divine. For example, the discovery that the universe is expanding has led many to speculate about the nature of creation. If the universe is not static but dynamic, constantly growing and changing, what does this say about the nature of God? Could God be an evolving force, one that grows and changes along with the universe?

Similarly, the discovery of *exoplanets*—planets orbiting other stars—has raised questions about the existence of life beyond Earth. If life exists elsewhere in the universe, how does this affect our understanding of the divine? Does God care for all living beings, regardless of where they are in the universe? Or is humanity unique in its relationship with the divine?

These questions highlight the intersection of science and spirituality, reminding us that scientific discoveries often lead to deeper spiritual questions. As we learn more about the universe, we are forced to confront the mysteries of existence and our place within the cosmos.

The Unity of Science and Spirituality

While science and spirituality may approach the universe from different perspectives, they are ultimately united in their quest for truth. Both seek to understand the nature of reality, the origins of the universe, and the role of consciousness in creation. And both offer valuable insights into the mysteries of.

In many ways, science and spirituality are two sides of the same coin. Science explores the *how* of the universe—how it works, how it came into being, and how it evolves. Spirituality, on the other hand, explores the *why*—why the universe exists, why we are here, and what our purpose is. Together, they provide a more complete understanding of the universe, one that embraces both the material and the metaphysical.

As we move forward in our exploration of the cosmos, it is important to recognize the value of both science and spirituality. By integrating these two perspectives, we can gain a deeper understanding of the universe and our place within it. The intersection of science and spirituality offers us a unique opportunity to explore the mysteries of existence, to seek both knowledge and meaning, and to embrace the wonder and awe that the universe inspires.

Conclusion: A Unified Path to Understanding

In this chapter, we have explored the intersection of science and spirituality, examining how these two approaches complement one another in the search for truth. While science reveals the mechanics of the universe, spirituality offers insight into its deeper meaning. Together, they provide a more complete understanding of the cosmos, one that embraces both the material and the metaphysical.

As we continue our journey through the universe, we will explore the deeper implications of this unity, seeking to understand how science and spirituality can work together to uncover the mysteries of existence. The universe invites us to look beyond the surface, to explore both the visible and the invisible, and to seek meaning in the vastness of creation.

Chapter 8 concludes.

Chapter 9

Chapter 9: The Multiverse and Infinite Creation

A Universe Among Many

For centuries, humans have gazed at the stars, wondering about the nature of the universe. Are we alone in the cosmos? Is our universe the only one, or could there be countless other universes beyond our own? These questions have long fascinated scientists and philosophers alike, and in recent years, the idea of the *multiverse*—a collection of multiple, possibly infinite, universes—has gained traction as a serious scientific theory.

The multiverse theory challenges our understanding of reality, suggesting that our universe may be just one of many, each with its own unique laws of physics, constants, and forms of matter. In some universes, the physical conditions may be radically different, while in others, they may be nearly identical to our own. The possibilities are endless, and the implications are profound.

In this chapter, we will explore the concept of the multiverse, examining the scientific evidence, the philosophical questions it raises, and the potential spiritual insights it offers. Could the multiverse be a reflection of infinite creation, a testament to the boundless creativity of the divine? Or is it a purely scientific phenomenon, one that reveals the vast complexity of the cosmos?

The Many Worlds of Quantum Mechanics

One of the earliest scientific theories to suggest the existence of a multiverse comes from *quantum mechanics*, the branch of physics that deals with the behavior of particles on the smallest scales. In the quantum world, particles can exist in multiple states at once, a phenomenon known as *superposition*. When a particle is observed, it seems to "collapse" into a single state, but the question remains: What happens to the other possible states?

The *Many-Worlds Interpretation* of quantum mechanics suggests that every time a particle's state is observed, the universe splits into multiple branches, with each branch representing a different outcome. In this view, every possible outcome of a quantum event actually happens, but in separate, parallel universes. For example, if you flip a coin, in one universe it lands heads, while in another universe it lands tails. Both outcomes are real, but they occur in different worlds.

This idea of parallel universes, each representing a different version of reality, raises profound questions about the nature of choice, free will, and the structure of the cosmos. Could there be countless versions of ourselves, each living out a different set of possibilities? If so, what does this mean for our understanding of identity, consciousness, and the meaning of life?

Cosmic Inflation and the Bubble Multiverse

Another scientific theory that supports the idea of a multiverse comes from *cosmic inflation*, the rapid expansion of the universe that occurred in the first fractions of a second after the Big Bang. According to inflation theory, different regions of space may have experienced inflation at different rates, leading to the formation of separate "bubble universes." Each of these bubbles could be a distinct universe, with its own unique properties and laws of physics.

In the *Bubble Multiverse* model, our universe is just one of many bubbles floating in a vast, higher-dimensional space. Some bubbles may contain universes like ours, while others may be completely alien, with laws of physics that are unrecognizable to us. The bubble universes are not connected by space or time, meaning that travel between them is impossible, but they all exist simultaneously, side by side in the multiverse.

This model suggests that the multiverse is not just a theoretical concept but a natural consequence of the laws of physics. If inflation is true, then the multiverse may be an inevitable part of the cosmos, with new universes constantly being born as inflation continues in other regions of space.

Infinite Possibilities: The Nature of Creation in the Multiverse

The multiverse theory raises profound questions about the nature of creation. If there are infinite universes, each with its own unique properties, what does this say about the nature of the cosmos and the role of a creator? In some spiritual traditions, the multiverse is seen as a reflection of divine creativity, an expression of the boundless potential of the divine mind.

In Hinduism, for example, the universe is said to go through cycles of creation and destruction, with each cycle giving rise to new forms of life and consciousness. The idea of infinite creation is also found in other spiritual traditions, such as Kabbalah, which teaches that the divine light creates an infinite number of worlds, each reflecting a different aspect of the divine.

From this perspective, the multiverse is not just a scientific theory but a testament to the infinite creativity of the universe. Each universe in the multiverse is a unique creation, a different expression of the same underlying reality. The multiverse suggests that creation is not a one-time event but an ongoing process, one that continues to unfold in countless different ways.

The Anthropic Principle: Why Is Our Universe Special?

One of the most intriguing aspects of the multiverse theory is the idea that our universe may be just one of many, yet it seems uniquely suited for life. This raises the question: Why does our universe have the precise conditions necessary for life to exist? This question is often addressed through the *Anthropic Principle*, which suggests that the universe must have the conditions necessary for life, because if it didn't, we wouldn't be here to observe it.

In a multiverse, there could be countless other universes with different physical constants, most of which would not be suitable for life. Our universe may be special simply because it happens to have the right conditions for life to emerge. In other words, we live in a universe that is "fine-tuned" for life, but this fine-tuning may be the result of random chance in a multiverse filled with countless other, lifeless universes.

The Anthropic Principle raises deep philosophical questions about the nature of existence. Is our universe the product of chance, or is there a deeper reason why life exists? Is the multiverse a reflection of divine intention, or is it a purely natural phenomenon, governed by the laws of physics?

The Mystery of Parallel Universes: Spiritual and Scientific Insights

The idea of parallel universes is not just a scientific concept; it has been a part of spiritual and philosophical traditions for millennia. In many cultures, the idea of multiple realms of existence is central to their understanding of the cosmos. In Buddhism, for example, the concept of *multiple worlds* suggests that there are countless realms of existence, each inhabited by different beings with different levels of consciousness.

Similarly, in many indigenous traditions, the physical world is seen as just one layer of reality, with other, unseen realms existing alongside it. These parallel realms are often inhabited by spirits, ancestors, or gods, and they are believed to influence the physical world in subtle and mysterious ways.

The scientific concept of the multiverse echoes these ancient spiritual ideas, suggesting that there may be countless parallel realities, each existing simultaneously with our own. Whether viewed through the lens of science or spirituality, the multiverse invites us to consider the possibility that reality is far more complex and layered than we can perceive.

The Divine Play: Creation, Destruction, and Rebirth in the Multiverse

In many spiritual traditions, the universe is seen as a cycle of creation, destruction, and rebirth. In Hinduism, this cycle is represented by the *Trimurti*—the three gods Brahma (the creator), Vishnu (the preserver), and Shiva (the destroyer). The universe is constantly being created, preserved, and destroyed, with each cycle giving rise to new forms of life and consciousness.

The multiverse theory reflects this idea of cosmic cycles on a grand scale. In the multiverse, universes are constantly being born and dying, each one a unique creation with its own destiny. Some universes may last for billions of years, while others may collapse in an instant. But the process of creation and destruction is never-ending, as new universes are continually being born in the multiverse.

This idea of cosmic cycles suggests that the multiverse is not a static structure but a dynamic, evolving system. The birth and death of universes are part of a larger process of cosmic evolution, one that mirrors the cycles of creation and destruction found in many spiritual traditions.

The Implications of the Multiverse for Understanding God

If the multiverse is real, what does it mean for our understanding of God? In some interpretations, the multiverse suggests that God's creativity is infinite, extending beyond the boundaries of a single universe. Each universe in the multiverse could be seen as a unique expression of the divine, a different aspect of creation that reflects the boundless potential of the cosmos.

The multiverse also raises questions about the nature of divine intention. If there are infinite universes, each with its own laws of physics and forms of life, does God have a unique plan for each one? Or is the multiverse a reflection of free will, with each universe unfolding according to its own internal logic?

These questions challenge traditional notions of God as a creator with a specific plan for the universe. Instead, the multiverse suggests a more expansive view of the divine—one that embraces the infinite possibilities of creation and the idea that reality itself is a reflection of divine creativity.

Conclusion: Embracing the Infinite

The multiverse theory challenges our understanding of the universe, suggesting that our reality may be just one of countless others. Whether viewed through the lens of science or spirituality, the multiverse invites us to contemplate the infinite possibilities of creation, the boundless creativity of the divine, and the mystery of existence itself.

As we continue our journey through the cosmos, we will explore the deeper implications of the multiverse and what it means for our understanding of life, consciousness, and the divine. The multiverse opens the door to infinite possibilities, where each universe is a new creation, a new reality, shaped by different laws and forces. It reminds us that the universe we inhabit is just one piece of a far grander puzzle, a single thread in a vast cosmic tapestry.

Whether or not the multiverse is real, it forces us to expand our vision of the universe, to embrace the idea that reality is far more complex and vaster than we can comprehend. And in doing so, it offers us a deeper appreciation for the mystery and beauty of creation—both seen and unseen, both known and unknown.

Chapter 9 concludes.

Chapter 10: Consciousness and the Universe

The Awakening of Awareness

From the moment we are born, we begin to experience the world through the lens of consciousness. It is through our consciousness that we perceive reality, form thoughts, and cultivate awareness of ourselves and the universe around us. But what is consciousness, and how does it fit into the grand design of the cosmos? Could it be that consciousness is not merely a product of the brain, but a fundamental aspect of the universe itself?

In this chapter, we will explore the relationship between consciousness and the universe. We will delve into the mysteries of self-awareness, the interconnectedness of all things, and the possibility that consciousness plays a crucial role in shaping reality. By examining both scientific and spiritual perspectives, we will seek to understand how consciousness fits into the cosmic order and how it influences our understanding of existence.

The Mystery of Consciousness

Consciousness is one of the greatest mysteries of science and philosophy. Despite advances in neuroscience, we still do not fully understand how the brain generates conscious experience. What is it that gives rise to the feeling of self-awareness, the ability to think, perceive, and experience emotions? How can the electrical signals in our brain create the rich, subjective experience that we call consciousness?

Many scientists believe that consciousness is an emergent property of the brain—a by-product of the complex interactions between neurons. However, this explanation leaves many questions unanswered. Why do we experience the world in the way that we do? Why do we have a sense of self, an "I" that seems to observe our thoughts and emotions?

Some theorists argue that consciousness cannot be fully explained by the physical processes of the brain alone. Instead, they propose that consciousness is a fundamental aspect of the universe, much like space, time, and matter. This idea, known as *panpsychism*, suggests that consciousness is present in all things, from the smallest particles to the largest galaxies. In this view, the universe is not a lifeless machine but a living, conscious entity, with awareness permeating every level of existence.

Consciousness and Quantum Physics

One of the most intriguing intersections between consciousness and science is found in the field of *quantum physics*. At the quantum level, particles behave in ways that defy our everyday understanding of reality. They can exist in multiple states at once, become entangled across vast distances, and seem to "choose" a state only when they are observed. This phenomenon has led some scientists to speculate that consciousness plays a role in shaping the behavior of particles.

The famous *double-slit experiment* in quantum mechanics demonstrates this strange relationship between observation and reality. When particles, such as electrons or photons, are fired at a barrier with two slits, they behave as waves, creating an interference pattern on a detector. However, when the particles are observed, they behave like particles, passing through only one slit and creating two distinct lines on the detector. This suggests that the mere act of observation can change the outcome of the experiment, raising the possibility that consciousness influences the behavior of matter.

While this interpretation of quantum mechanics is controversial, it opens up fascinating questions about the nature of reality and the role of consciousness. Could it be that consciousness is not just a passive observer but an active participant in the unfolding of the universe? If so, what does this mean for our understanding of the relationship between mind and matter?

The Interconnectedness of Consciousness

Another important aspect of consciousness is its interconnectedness with the universe. Many spiritual traditions teach that all beings are connected through a shared consciousness, a universal mind that transcends individual awareness. This idea is central to philosophies such as Hinduism, where the concept of *Brahman* represents the ultimate reality, a divine consciousness that pervades all things.

In modern science, this interconnectedness is reflected in the study of ecosystems and the web of life. Just as every living organism is connected to its environment, every part of the universe is connected through physical forces such as gravity and electromagnetism. But the connections between living beings may go beyond the physical. Some researchers in the field of *consciousness studies* suggest that consciousness itself may be a shared phenomenon, one that connects all living beings in ways we do not yet fully understand.

The idea of a universal consciousness raises profound questions about the nature of individuality and the self. If consciousness is interconnected, where do we draw the line between the self and the rest of the universe? Are we truly separate from the world around us, or are we part of a larger, cosmic awareness that transcends our individual minds?

The Role of Consciousness in Creation

If consciousness is indeed a fundamental aspect of the universe, then it may play a crucial role in the process of creation. In many spiritual traditions, consciousness is seen as the creative force behind the universe. The divine mind, or *logos*, is believed to shape reality through its thoughts, just as we shape our personal experiences through our own thoughts and perceptions.

In Hinduism, for example, the universe is said to be the product of *Brahma's* thoughts, with reality unfolding as a manifestation of divine consciousness. In Christianity, the concept of the *Word* (or *logos*) represents the creative power of God, through which the universe was brought into being. These traditions suggest that consciousness is not just a passive observer of reality but an active creator, shaping the universe through thought and intention.

This idea aligns with modern interpretations of quantum mechanics, which suggest that consciousness may influence the behavior of particles and, by extension, the structure of reality itself. If consciousness plays a role in shaping the universe, then it may be that our thoughts and intentions have a direct impact on the world around us. This raises profound questions about the power of the mind and the relationship between consciousness and creation.

Exploring Higher States of Consciousness

Throughout history, many individuals have reported experiences of higher states of consciousness—moments of deep spiritual insight, profound clarity, and a sense of connection to the universe. These experiences often occur during meditation, near-death experiences, or under the influence of certain substances, and they are characterized by a feeling of unity with the cosmos and a sense of transcending ordinary reality.

In these higher states of consciousness, individuals often describe a sense of oneness with the universe, a feeling that they are part of something much larger than themselves. They may experience a dissolution of the ego, or the sense of individual self, and an awareness of a deeper, universal consciousness that pervades all things.

These experiences suggest that consciousness may not be limited to the everyday waking state but may have the capacity to expand and explore higher dimensions of reality. Spiritual traditions such as Buddhism, Hinduism, and Sufism emphasize the importance of cultivating higher states of consciousness through meditation, prayer, and contemplation. By transcending the limitations of ordinary awareness, individuals may gain insight into the true nature of reality and their place within the cosmos.

The Future of Consciousness Exploration

As science continues to explore the mysteries of consciousness, new technologies and techniques may allow us to probe deeper into the nature of the mind and its relationship to the universe. Already, advances in neuroscience, artificial intelligence, and virtual reality are expanding our understanding of consciousness and offering new ways to experience reality.

In the future, we may develop technologies that allow us to enhance our consciousness, explore altered states of awareness, and even connect our minds to other forms of consciousness. These advances could revolutionize our understanding of the self, the universe, and the nature of existence.

At the same time, spiritual practices such as meditation, mindfulness, and yoga continue to offer powerful tools for exploring consciousness. By cultivating awareness and expanding our understanding of the mind, we can deepen our connection to the universe and unlock the full potential of our consciousness.

Conclusion: Consciousness and the Cosmos

Consciousness is the lens through which we experience reality, the bridge between the self and the universe. Whether viewed through the lens of science or spirituality, consciousness remains one of the greatest mysteries of existence, raising profound questions about the nature of reality, the interconnectedness of all things, and the role of the mind in shaping the cosmos.

As we continue our journey through the universe, we will explore the deeper implications of consciousness and its relationship to creation, life, and the divine. The universe invites us to explore not only the outer world but also the inner world of the mind, where the mysteries of existence unfold in the light of awareness.

Chapter 10 concludes.

92

Chapter 11

Chapter 11: Life Beyond Earth—The Cosmic Dance of Evolution

Life's Origins: Earth as a Starting Point

Our planet, Earth, is a unique cradle of life. Over billions of years, life evolved from the simplest microorganisms to the complex forms we see today, including humans. The conditions on Earth—its atmosphere, distance from the Sun, and abundance of water—provided the perfect environment for life to flourish. But as we explore the universe, the question arises: Could life exist elsewhere? And if so, how does life emerge and evolve in different corners of the cosmos?

In this chapter, we will explore the possibility of life beyond Earth, examining the factors that make life possible and the potential for life to evolve on other planets. We will delve into the scientific search for extra-terrestrial life, the philosophical implications of discovering life elsewhere, and the spiritual significance of life as a fundamental force in the universe. As we journey through the cosmos, we will contemplate the possibility that life is not a rare anomaly but a natural outcome of the universe's creative processes.

The Ingredients for Life: A Universal Recipe?

Life, as we know it, depends on several key ingredients: water, carbon, and energy. On Earth, these ingredients combined in the primordial oceans, where simple molecules formed the building blocks of life.

Over time, these molecules evolved into more complex forms, eventually giving rise to the first living cells.

The same conditions that allowed life to emerge on Earth could exist on other planets. Scientists have identified thousands of *exoplanets*—planets orbiting stars outside our solar system—and many of these planets lie within the *habitable zone*, where conditions might be right for liquid water to exist. Some exoplanets are even Earth-like, with atmospheres that could support life.

But what if life doesn't need the same ingredients as life on Earth? Some scientists speculate that life could exist in forms radically different from anything we've encountered. For example, life could be based on silicon instead of carbon, or it could thrive in environments that are toxic to us, such as methane-rich atmospheres or icy moons with subsurface oceans.

The diversity of planetary environments in the universe suggests that life could take on many forms, adapting to the unique conditions of each world. Life may not be a rare occurrence, but a natural consequence of the universe's inherent creativity.

The Search for Extra-terrestrial Life

For decades, scientists have been searching for signs of life beyond Earth. One of the most ambitious projects is the *Search for Extra-terrestrial Intelligence* (SETI), which uses radio telescopes to listen for signals from intelligent civilizations. While no definitive signals have been detected so far, the search continues, driven by the belief that we are not alone in the universe.

NASA's exploration of planets and moons in our solar system has also yielded tantalizing clues. Mars, once a dry and barren world, may have had liquid water on its surface in the past, and some researchers believe that microbial life could still exist beneath the surface. Europa, one of Jupiter's moons, has a subsurface ocean that could harbor life, while Saturn's moon Enceladus has geysers that spew water and organic molecules into space.

These discoveries suggest that life may be more common than we previously thought, even within our own solar system. If life can exist on Mars, Europa, or Enceladus, then it could also exist on countless other worlds throughout the galaxy.

The Cosmic Dance of Evolution

Life on Earth has followed a long and winding path of evolution, driven by the forces of natural selection, adaptation, and environmental change. From the first single-celled organisms to the diversity of species we see today, life has constantly evolved to meet the challenges of survival. But what if this process of evolution is not limited to Earth? Could the same forces of evolution be at work on other planets, shaping life in ways we can only imagine?

The principles of evolution are universal, and they suggest that life on other planets, if it exists, would follow a similar path. Organisms would adapt to their environments, developing new traits to survive and thrive. On a planet with high gravity, for example, life forms might evolve to be shorter and sturdier. On a planet with a dense atmosphere, organisms might develop different ways of breathing or absorbing nutrients.

The diversity of life on Earth offers a glimpse into the potential diversity of life in the universe. Just as life on Earth has evolved into countless forms, from bacteria to whales to humans, life on other planets could take on an infinite variety of shapes and forms, each uniquely adapted to its environment.

The Spiritual Significance of Life in the Universe

The discovery of life beyond Earth would have profound spiritual implications. For centuries, humanity has wondered whether we are alone in the universe. If we were to discover life elsewhere, it would challenge our understanding of our place in the cosmos and our relationship with the divine.

Many spiritual traditions teach that life is a sacred gift, a reflection of the divine spark that animates the universe. In Christianity, life is seen as a creation of God, with each living being possessing a soul. In Hinduism and Buddhism, life is part of the cycle of birth, death, and rebirth, with all living beings interconnected through the web of existence.

If life exists elsewhere in the universe, it suggests that the divine spark is not limited to Earth but is present throughout the cosmos. Life, in this view, is not a random accident but a fundamental force that pervades the universe, connecting all living beings in a cosmic dance of creation and evolution.

The Potential for Intelligent Life

One of the most intriguing questions in the search for extra-terrestrial life is whether intelligent civilizations exist elsewhere in the universe.

The *Fermi Paradox* highlights the apparent contradiction between the high probability of intelligent life in the universe and the lack of evidence for it. If intelligent civilizations are common, why haven't we detected any signs of them?

There are many possible explanations for the Fermi Paradox. Perhaps intelligent civilizations are rare, or they are too far away for us to detect. It's also possible that advanced civilizations use communication methods that we don't yet understand, or that they deliberately avoid contact with less advanced species like ours.

The discovery of intelligent life would force us to rethink our understanding of civilization, culture, and consciousness. How would we communicate with beings from another world? What moral and ethical responsibilities would we have toward them? And how would their existence reshape our understanding of humanity's role in the universe?

The Future of Life in the Cosmos

As we look to the future, the question of life beyond Earth becomes increasingly relevant. Humanity is on the verge of becoming a spacefaring civilization, with plans to establish colonies on the Moon, Mars, and beyond. As we venture into the cosmos, we may encounter new forms of life, some similar to our own, others radically different.

The future of life in the universe is full of possibilities. Perhaps we will one day communicate with intelligent civilizations, learning from their wisdom and sharing our own. Perhaps we will discover microbial life on distant planets, offering new insights into the origins of life. Or perhaps we will seed life on other worlds, spreading Earth's biology across the cosmos and becoming creators in our own right.

The discovery of life beyond Earth would not only answer one of the most profound questions in science but also open up new avenues for spiritual exploration. It would invite us to see life as a cosmic force, one that transcends the boundaries of planets and galaxies, and connects all living beings in a grand, universal story of creation and evolution.

Conclusion: Life as a Cosmic Force

Life is one of the most remarkable phenomena in the universe. Whether it exists only on Earth or is spread throughout the cosmos, life is a testament to the creative power of the universe. It is a force that transcends the boundaries of planets, stars, and galaxies, connecting all living beings in a shared journey of evolution and discovery.

As we continue our search for life beyond Earth, we are reminded that life is not just a biological process but a cosmic dance, one that reflects the underlying order and creativity of the universe. Whether through science or spirituality, the search for life is a search for meaning, for connection, and for our place in the grand design of creation.

Chapter 11 concludes.

CHAPTER 12

Chapter 12: The Evolution of Intelligence and Technology Across the Cosmos

The Emergence of Intelligence

The evolution of intelligence is one of the most remarkable phenomena in the universe. From the earliest life forms on Earth to the development of advanced civilizations, intelligence has allowed living beings to understand their environment, adapt to new challenges, and create technologies that shape the world around them. But is intelligence a rare occurrence, or is it a natural outcome of evolution across the cosmos?

In this chapter, we will explore the evolution of intelligence and technology in the universe. We will examine how intelligence may have evolved on other planets, how advanced civilizations might develop, and how technology serves as both a tool and a reflection of the growth of consciousness. Through this lens, we will consider the possibility that the universe itself fosters the emergence of intelligence, guiding it toward greater complexity and interconnectedness.

From Tools to Technology: The Growth of Intelligence

On Earth, the development of intelligence is closely linked to the use of tools and the creation of technology. Early humans learned to use simple tools—stones, sticks, and fire—to manipulate their environment, and over time, these tools became more sophisticated.

As intelligence evolved, so too did the ability to create technologies that transformed the world, from agriculture to cities, from the wheel to the internet.

But the story of intelligence and technology is not limited to Earth. In a universe filled with billions of planets, it is likely that intelligent life has emerged elsewhere, each civilization developing its own unique technologies. Some may be primitive, using simple tools to hunt and gather, while others may have achieved levels of technological advancement far beyond our own, mastering the ability to travel between stars, harness unlimited energy, or even manipulate the fabric of space-time itself.

The progression from simple tools to advanced technologies reflects a deeper process of evolution, one in which intelligence continuously expands its understanding of the universe and its ability to shape reality. This process may be universal, unfolding on countless planets across the cosmos, each civilization moving along its own path of discovery and innovation.

Technological Civilizations: The Kardashev Scale

One way to understand the progression of intelligence and technology is through the *Kardashev Scale*, a system developed by the Soviet astronomer Nikolai Kardashev in 1964. The scale measures a civilization's technological advancement based on its ability to harness and use energy, dividing civilizations into three categories:

- **Type I Civilization**: A civilization that has harnessed all the energy available on its home planet, using resources such as wind, solar, and geothermal energy. Earth is approaching this level of civilization, as we begin to explore renewable energy sources and develop technologies to manage the planet's resources more efficiently.

- **Type II Civilization**: A civilization that can harness the energy of its entire star, using structures such as *Dyson spheres*—hypothetical megastructures that capture the energy output of a star. Such a civilization would have the technological ability to build massive space stations, travel between planets, and control the energy needs of its entire solar system.

- **Type III Civilization**: A civilization that has harnessed the energy of its entire galaxy, using advanced technologies to manipulate stars, black holes, and other cosmic phenomena. These civilizations would be capable of intergalactic travel, possibly exploring and colonizing distant galaxies.

The Kardashev Scale offers a glimpse into the potential future of intelligent civilizations, suggesting that as intelligence evolves, so too does the ability to control and utilize the vast resources of the universe. While humanity is still far from reaching even Type I status, the scale raises the possibility that other civilizations in the cosmos may have already achieved far greater levels of technological mastery.

The Impact of Technology on Consciousness

Technology is not just a tool for survival; it also shapes the way we think, perceive, and understand the universe. As civilizations develop more advanced technologies, they also expand their consciousness, exploring new realms of possibility and gaining deeper insights into the nature of existence.

For example, the invention of the telescope allowed humans to see beyond the boundaries of Earth, revealing the vastness of the cosmos and challenging our understanding of the universe. The development of computers and the internet has connected people across the globe, creating a global consciousness that allows for the sharing of knowledge, ideas, and culture. And as we venture into space, new technologies will enable us to explore distant planets and galaxies, expanding our understanding of life and the cosmos.

But technology also raises important ethical and philosophical questions. How should we use our technological abilities? What responsibilities do we have toward other civilizations, both on Earth and in the cosmos? As we develop more advanced technologies, we must also cultivate a deeper sense of wisdom and responsibility, ensuring that our creations serve the greater good and foster the continued evolution of consciousness.

Artificial Intelligence: The Next Stage of Evolution?

As technology evolves, so too does the potential for the emergence of *artificial intelligence* (AI)—machines and systems that possess intelligence comparable to, or even surpassing, that of humans. AI has the potential to revolutionize every aspect of life, from medicine to transportation to communication. But it also raises profound questions about the nature of intelligence and the future of humanity.

Some scientists and futurists speculate that AI could represent the next stage of evolution, with machines becoming conscious entities capable of independent thought and creativity. In this scenario, humans may merge with machines, creating a hybrid form of intelligence that combines the best of biological and artificial systems. This idea, often referred to as the *singularity*, suggests that the boundaries between human and machine, and between biology and technology, may one day blur.

But the rise of AI also raises concerns about the potential consequences of creating machines that surpass human intelligence. Could AI become a threat to humanity, as depicted in science fiction? Or could it become a powerful ally, helping us solve the greatest challenges of our time, from climate change to space exploration?

The Ethical Challenges of Technological Advancement

With the evolution of intelligence and technology comes a host of ethical challenges. How should we manage the impact of technology on society, the environment, and the universe? What responsibilities do we have toward future generations and other intelligent civilizations?

One of the greatest ethical challenges is the potential for technological inequality. As advanced technologies become more prevalent, there is a risk that access to these technologies will be concentrated in the hands of a few, leading to greater disparities between wealthy and poor civilizations. Ensuring that technology is used for the benefit of all, rather than a select few, will be a key challenge for the future.

Another ethical challenge is the potential for technology to alter the environment, both on Earth and in space. As we explore other planets and develop new technologies, we must be mindful of the impact on ecosystems and the broader cosmic environment. The preservation of life, both human and non-human, must remain a central priority in our technological endeavors.

Technology and the Future of Cosmic Civilization

As intelligence and technology continue to evolve, the future of civilization may lie in the stars. Humanity is already taking its first steps toward becoming a spacefaring civilization, with plans to establish colonies on the Moon, Mars, and beyond. As we venture further into space, we may encounter other intelligent civilizations, each with its own technological advancements and ways of understanding the universe.

The future of cosmic civilization is full of possibilities. Perhaps we will one day establish vast networks of communication and trade between different planets and galaxies, creating a cosmic community of intelligent beings. Perhaps we will develop technologies that allow us to travel faster than light, exploring the farthest reaches of the universe. Or perhaps we will transcend the limitations of physical space and time, unlocking new dimensions of existence through the power of consciousness and technology.

Whatever the future holds, the evolution of intelligence and technology will play a central role in shaping the destiny of life in the universe.

Conclusion: The Cosmic Journey of Intelligence

The evolution of intelligence and technology is a cosmic journey, one that reflects the underlying creativity and complexity of the universe. From the first use of tools to the development of advanced spacefaring civilizations, intelligence has allowed living beings to explore, understand, and shape the world around them. As technology continues to evolve, it will open up new possibilities for life, consciousness, and the future of civilization in the cosmos. The universe invites us to embrace the potential of intelligence, to use our technological abilities for the greater good, and to explore the mysteries of existence with wisdom and responsibility. The journey of intelligence is far from over, and as we look to the stars, we are reminded that the possibilities are truly infinite.

Chapter 12 concludes.

CHAPTER 13

Chapter 13: Humanity's Future as a Cosmic Civilization

The Next Great Frontier

Humanity has always been driven by exploration, from the early days of discovering new lands on Earth to the bold steps of space exploration. As we look to the future, the next great frontier is the cosmos itself. Our technological advancements, combined with our desire to explore and expand, will lead humanity toward becoming a *cosmic civilization*—a species that ventures beyond its home planet to settle and thrive among the stars.

In this chapter, we will explore humanity's potential future as a spacefaring civilization. We will examine the technological and societal shifts that will be necessary to build human colonies on other planets, the challenges and opportunities of interstellar travel, and the possibility of interacting with other intelligent species. The journey from a planetary civilization to a cosmic one will not only reshape our understanding of the universe but also redefine what it means to be human.

Building Human Colonies on Other Planets

The first step toward becoming a cosmic civilization is establishing human colonies on other planets. Mars has long been the focus of space exploration, with NASA and private companies like SpaceX working toward the goal of sending humans to the Red Planet.

Colonizing Mars will be a monumental achievement, requiring advancements in space travel, life support systems, and sustainable habitats.

Mars, with its relatively hospitable environment compared to other planets, will serve as humanity's first outpost in the cosmos. But the challenges are immense: the thin atmosphere, harsh temperatures, and lack of liquid water on the surface make it a difficult place to live. To overcome these challenges, scientists and engineers are developing technologies such as *closed-loop life support systems*, which recycle air, water, and waste to sustain human life, and *terraforming* techniques, which could potentially transform the planet's environment over centuries to make it more Earth-like.

But Mars is only the beginning. As our technologies improve, humanity may establish colonies on moons such as Europa or Titan, or even create floating habitats in the upper atmospheres of gas giants like Venus. These colonies will not be mere scientific outposts but fully functioning societies, where humans live, work, and build new cultures that reflect the unique environments of their new homes.

Interstellar Travel: Reaching the Stars

While colonizing planets within our solar system is a significant step, the true mark of a cosmic civilization is the ability to travel between stars. Interstellar travel, once the domain of science fiction, may one day become a reality as we develop new propulsion technologies that can take us beyond the limits of our solar system.

Current spacecraft are far too slow to reach even the nearest stars within a human lifetime. To make interstellar travel possible, we will need to develop *breakthrough propulsion systems*—technologies such as *nuclear fusion, antimatter engines*, or even the speculative *warp drives* that could allow us to travel faster than the speed of light by bending space-time.

Reaching other star systems opens up the possibility of discovering new planets that may be even more suitable for colonization than Mars. The search for *exoplanets*—planets orbiting other stars—has already identified many Earth-like candidates within the habitable zones of their stars. These planets could one day become homes for human settlers, expanding humanity's reach across the galaxy.

The Challenges of Cosmic Expansion

Becoming a cosmic civilization will not be without its challenges. One of the greatest hurdles is the sheer distance between stars. Even with advanced propulsion technologies, interstellar travel will require massive investments of time, energy, and resources. Establishing self-sustaining colonies on distant planets will also require breakthroughs in *automation, artificial intelligence*, and *robotics* to ensure that colonies can function independently of Earth for long periods.

Another challenge is the potential for social and cultural fragmentation. As humans spread out across different planets and star systems, communication between colonies may become difficult due to the vast distances involved. This could lead to the development of isolated societies with distinct cultures, languages, and technologies. Maintaining a sense of unity and cooperation among these far-flung colonies will be essential for the survival of the cosmic civilization.

Additionally, the ethical implications of cosmic expansion must be considered. How should humanity interact with any alien life forms it encounters? What responsibilities do we have toward the planets and ecosystems we colonize? As we expand into the cosmos, we must develop ethical frameworks that ensure our actions promote peace, sustainability, and respect for other forms of life.

Interacting with Other Intelligent Species

One of the most profound possibilities of becoming a cosmic civilization is the chance to encounter other intelligent species. The discovery of extra-terrestrial life, particularly intelligent life, would be one of the most significant events in human history, forcing us to rethink our place in the universe and our understanding of civilization.

The *Fermi Paradox*, which questions why we have not yet detected any signs of intelligent life despite the vastness of the universe, suggests that either intelligent civilizations are exceedingly rare, or they are deliberately avoiding contact with us. If we do encounter other civilizations, the implications will be vast, raising questions about how we communicate, trade, and coexist with beings that may have entirely different cultures, technologies, and values.

Interstellar diplomacy will require us to develop new forms of communication, perhaps using mathematics or physics as a universal language. We will also need to navigate the ethical complexities of interacting with civilizations that may be more or less advanced than our own. The discovery of intelligent life would open up new possibilities for collaboration, exploration, and mutual growth, but it could also present risks, particularly if those civilizations have goals that conflict with our own.

The Cultural Evolution of a Cosmic Civilization

As humanity spreads across the cosmos, our culture will evolve in ways we cannot yet predict. The cultures of Earth, shaped by geography, history, and shared experiences, may diverge as humans settle on different planets and encounter new environments. Colonies on Mars may develop distinct traditions, art forms, and philosophies that reflect the harsh, alien landscape of their new home, while space farers living in orbital habitats may develop a culture centered on technology and life in the void.

At the same time, the vast distances between colonies may challenge the idea of a shared human identity. To maintain a sense of unity as a species, humanity will need to cultivate a cosmic culture—one that transcends the boundaries of planets and star systems, embracing the diversity of human experiences while fostering a shared vision for the future.

Art, music, literature, and philosophy will play crucial roles in this cultural evolution. As we encounter new worlds and possibly new civilizations, our creative expressions will reflect the wonder, challenges, and discoveries of life as a cosmic civilization. In this way, culture will continue to be a driving force in humanity's exploration of the universe, helping us navigate the unknown and find meaning in the vastness of space.

The Role of Consciousness in Cosmic Civilization

As humanity becomes a cosmic civilization, the evolution of

consciousness will play an increasingly important role. The expansion of intelligence and technology will not only reshape our physical existence but also deepen our understanding of consciousness and its connection to the universe. As we explore new worlds and encounter new forms of life, we may gain insights into the nature of consciousness that transcend the limits of human experience.

Some futurists and philosophers believe that humanity's cosmic expansion will lead to a greater integration of consciousness with technology, creating new forms of intelligence that blend biological and artificial systems. This could result in *post-human* civilizations where consciousness is no longer confined to individual bodies but exists in networks of minds, connected across vast distances by advanced technologies.

The exploration of consciousness will also lead to new spiritual and philosophical insights. As we venture into the cosmos, we may develop new understandings of our place in the universe, our connection to other forms of life, and the deeper meaning of existence. The journey to become a cosmic civilization will not only be a physical one but also a journey of the mind and spirit.

The Future of Humanity in the Cosmos

The future of humanity as a cosmic civilization is filled with possibilities. As we continue to develop the technologies and capabilities needed to explore the universe, we will unlock new opportunities for discovery, innovation, and growth. The challenges of space exploration and colonization will push us to expand our understanding of science, technology, and ethics, while the potential to encounter other civilizations will challenge us to rethink our place in the cosmic order.

Humanity's future in the cosmos is not just about survival; it is about thriving, evolving, and embracing the full potential of life and intelligence in the universe. As we look to the stars, we are reminded that the universe is vast, filled with possibilities, and that our journey is only just beginning.

Conclusion: Humanity's Cosmic Destiny

As humanity takes its place among the stars, we will embark on a journey that will shape the future of our species and the universe itself. Becoming a cosmic civilization is not just a technological achievement but a profound evolution of consciousness, culture, and identity. It will require us to overcome challenges, embrace diversity, and work together as a species to explore the infinite possibilities of the cosmos. The universe invites us to explore, to expand, and to evolve. As we take our first steps toward becoming a cosmic civilization, we are reminded that our potential is as limitless as the stars themselves. The future is vast, and the possibilities are infinite.

Chapter 13 concludes

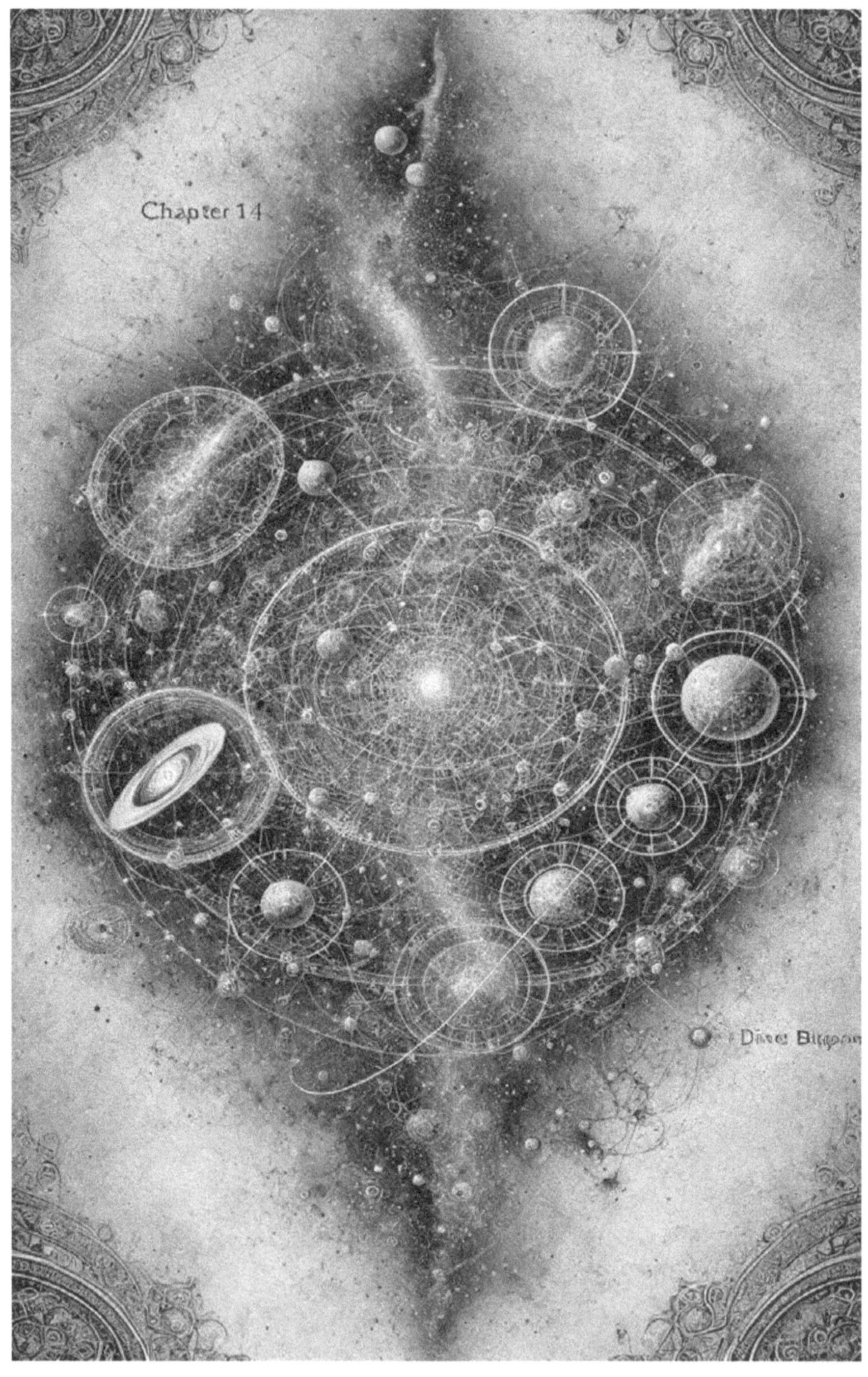
Chapter 14
Dwarf Bygone

Chapter 14: The Ethical Dimensions of Cosmic Exploration

The Ethics of Expanding into Space

As humanity sets its sights on the stars, ethical considerations become crucial in guiding our actions and decisions. The exploration and colonization of space present unique challenges that require us to reflect on our responsibilities and the potential consequences of our actions. This chapter delves into the ethical dimensions of cosmic exploration, exploring the moral frameworks that should guide our ventures into the universe.

The ethical questions surrounding space exploration are complex and multifaceted. They involve considerations of how we interact with other celestial bodies, the potential impacts on extra-terrestrial environments, and the implications of our actions for future generations. To navigate these ethical challenges, we must develop principles that ensure our activities in space promote the well-being of all forms of life and the preservation of the cosmos.

Preserving Celestial Environments

One of the primary ethical concerns in space exploration is the preservation of celestial environments. As we explore and potentially colonize other planets, we must be mindful of the impact our activities may have on these environments. Unlike Earth, which has been shaped by billions of years of natural processes, extra-terrestrial environments may be pristine and sensitive to human activities.

The concept of *planetary protection* involves safeguarding other planets and moons from contamination by Earth-based life forms, as well as preventing the spread of extra-terrestrial contaminants that could affect Earth. This is particularly important when exploring planets like Mars, where the search for microbial life is a key objective. Contaminating these environments with Earth-based microbes could jeopardize the integrity of scientific discoveries and the potential for future research.

Moreover, as we develop technologies for terraforming and colonization, we must consider the ethical implications of altering the environments of other planets. While terraforming may make planets more habitable for humans, it also raises questions about whether we have the right to change these environments and the potential consequences for any existing life forms.

Ethics of Interaction with Extra-terrestrial Life

The possibility of encountering extra-terrestrial life raises profound ethical questions. If we discover evidence of intelligent or microbial life beyond Earth, how should we approach these findings? The principles of *first contact* ethics suggest that we must act with caution, respect, and responsibility in our interactions with extra-terrestrial life.

The ethical framework for interacting with extra-terrestrial life should include considerations of non-interference, mutual respect, and the avoidance of exploitation. Just as we would expect others to respect our own sovereignty and rights, we must extend the same respect to any potential extra-terrestrial civilizations. The ethical principles of *cosmic stewardship* emphasize the importance of safeguarding the rights and well-being of all forms of life, regardless of their origin.

If we encounter advanced extra-terrestrial civilizations, we must carefully consider the implications of establishing communication and potentially engaging in exchanges of knowledge and technology. Ensuring that such interactions are conducted ethically and equitably will be essential for fostering positive and respectful relationships with other intelligent species.

Equity and Justice in Space Colonization

As humanity expands into space, issues of equity and justice become increasingly relevant. The development of space technologies and the establishment of space colonies have the potential to exacerbate existing inequalities or create new ones. Addressing these concerns requires a commitment to ensuring that the benefits of space exploration are shared fairly and that all people have an opportunity to participate in and benefit from these endeavors.

The distribution of resources and opportunities in space exploration must be managed to prevent the concentration of power and wealth in the hands of a few entities or nations. This involves creating frameworks for international cooperation and collaboration that ensure equitable access to space and its resources. The principles of *space law* and *space governance* are critical for establishing guidelines and agreements that promote fairness and prevent the exploitation of space for the benefit of a select few.

Moreover, as we develop new technologies and industries in space, we must consider their potential impact on social justice and human rights. Ensuring that space colonization efforts are conducted with respect for the rights and dignity of all individuals will be essential for building a just and equitable cosmic civilization.

The Responsibility to Future Generations

The decisions we make today about space exploration and colonization will have far-reaching consequences for future generations. As we venture into the cosmos, we bear a responsibility to ensure that our actions do not compromise the ability of future generations to thrive and explore.

The ethical principle of *intergenerational justice* emphasizes the importance of considering the long-term impacts of our decisions and ensuring that we leave a positive legacy for those who will come after us. This involves making choices that preserve the integrity of space environments, promote sustainable development, and uphold the values of fairness and respect for all forms of life.

Future generations will inherit the outcomes of our space exploration efforts, and it is our duty to ensure that we conduct these activities in a manner that benefits humanity as a whole. This includes fostering a culture of responsibility, accountability, and stewardship in our approach to space exploration and ensuring that our actions reflect the highest ethical standards.

Developing Ethical Frameworks for Cosmic Exploration

To navigate the ethical challenges of space exploration, we must develop robust ethical frameworks and guidelines that address the complexities of our cosmic endeavors. These frameworks should be informed by principles of respect, responsibility, and fairness and should involve input from diverse perspectives, including scientists, ethicists, policymakers, and the general public.

Creating ethical guidelines for space exploration involves addressing questions such as:

- How can we ensure the preservation of celestial environments and the protection of potential extra-terrestrial life?
- What principles should guide our interactions with intelligent or microbial extra-terrestrial life?
- How can we promote equity and justice in space colonization and ensure that the benefits of space exploration are shared fairly?
- What responsibilities do we have to future generations in terms of the long-term impacts of our space activities?

Developing comprehensive and inclusive ethical frameworks will be essential for guiding humanity's journey into the cosmos and ensuring that our exploration and colonization efforts are conducted with the highest regard for ethical principles and the well-being of all forms of life.

Conclusion: Embracing Ethical Responsibility

As we stand on the threshold of becoming a cosmic civilization, it is crucial to embrace our ethical responsibilities and approach space exploration with a deep sense of respect, caution, and fairness. The ethical dimensions of cosmic exploration are complex and multifaceted, requiring us to consider the preservation of celestial environments, the respectful interaction with extra-terrestrial life, and the promotion of equity and justice in our endeavours.

By developing and adhering to ethical frameworks that guide our actions in space, we can ensure that our journey into the cosmos reflects the best of humanity and contributes to a positive and sustainable future for all. The path to becoming a cosmic civilization is not only a journey of discovery and exploration but also a journey of ethical growth and responsibility.

Chapter 14 concludes.

Chapter 15

Chapter 15: The Cosmic Legacy of Humanity

The Vision of Humanity's Cosmic Future

As humanity looks to the stars, it must consider the legacy it wishes to leave behind. The exploration and colonization of space represent not only a technological and scientific achievement but also a profound shift in how we perceive our place in the universe. This chapter explores the concept of humanity's cosmic legacy, examining the aspirations, responsibilities, and potential impacts of our journey into the cosmos.

The vision of humanity's cosmic future involves a blend of ambition, imagination, and ethical considerations. It requires us to think deeply about what kind of civilization we want to become and how our actions today will shape the future of space exploration and colonization. Our cosmic legacy will be defined by the values we uphold, the decisions we make, and the impact we have on the universe and future generations.

The Aspirations of a Cosmic Civilization

Humanity's aspirations for a cosmic future are driven by a combination of curiosity, ambition, and the desire to expand beyond our earthly confines. These aspirations encompass a range of goals, including:

- **Exploration:** The quest to explore distant planets, moons, and star systems, driven by a desire to understand the universe and our place within it.
- **Colonization:** The establishment of human settlements beyond Earth, aimed at creating new habitats and ensuring the long-term survival of our species.
- **Innovation:** The development of advanced technologies and scientific breakthroughs that push the boundaries of what is possible and open new frontiers for exploration and discovery.
- **Sustainability:** The creation of sustainable practices and technologies that ensure the long-term viability of space settlements and minimize our impact on the environment.

These aspirations reflect humanity's deep-seated drive to explore the unknown and create a lasting impact on the cosmos. However, they also come with significant responsibilities and challenges that must be addressed to ensure that our cosmic endeavors are conducted ethically and with consideration   the broader implications.

Defining Our Cosmic Legacy

The concept of a cosmic legacy involves more than just technological achievements or scientific discoveries. It encompasses the values, principles, and cultural influences that we impart to future generations and other potential inhabitants of the cosmos. Key elements of humanity's cosmic legacy include:

- **Cultural Contributions:** The transmission of human culture, art, literature, and philosophy to future generations and potential extra-terrestrial civilizations. Our cultural legacy will shape how we are remembered and influence the development of new cosmic cultures.

- **Ethical Standards:** The establishment of ethical guidelines and practices that reflect our commitment to responsible exploration, respect for other forms of life, and the preservation of celestial environments. Our ethical legacy will serve as a model for future cosmic civilizations.

- **Scientific Knowledge:** The accumulation and dissemination of scientific knowledge that contributes to our understanding of the universe and advances the frontiers of human knowledge. Our scientific legacy will provide a foundation for future exploration and discovery.

- **Technological Innovations:** The development of technologies that revolutionize our ability to explore and inhabit space. Our technological legacy will drive progress and open new possibilities for future generations.

Defining our cosmic legacy requires a thoughtful and deliberate approach, ensuring that our actions and contributions reflect the best of humanity and have a positive impact on the universe.

The Responsibility of Cosmic Pioneers

As pioneers in the exploration and colonization of space, we bear a profound responsibility to ensure that our actions align with the highest standards of ethical conduct and respect for the cosmos. This responsibility includes:

- **Stewardship:** Taking care of the environments we explore and inhabit, and ensuring that our activities do not cause harm or irreversible damage. Stewardship involves both preserving the integrity of celestial bodies and fostering sustainable practices in space settlements.

- **Respect for Other Life Forms:** Approaching potential encounters with extra-terrestrial life with caution, respect, and a commitment to ethical principles. We must be mindful of the potential impacts of our actions on other forms of life and ensure that our interactions are conducted with integrity.
- **Preservation of Knowledge:** Safeguarding and transmitting scientific, cultural, and ethical knowledge to future generations and other cosmic civilizations. This involves creating systems for preserving and sharing information and ensuring that our legacy endures.

By embracing these responsibilities, we can ensure that our cosmic endeavors are conducted with the utmost respect for the universe and contribute to a positive and lasting legacy.

The Role of Education and Inspiration

Education and inspiration play a crucial role in shaping humanity's cosmic legacy. By fostering curiosity, creativity, and a sense of wonder about the universe, we can inspire future generations to pursue careers in space science and exploration and to contribute to the development of a cosmic civilization.

Educational initiatives should focus on:

- **Promoting Space Literacy:** Increasing public understanding of space science, exploration, and the ethical implications of cosmic endeavors. Space literacy helps individuals appreciate the significance of our cosmic aspirations and the challenges involved.

- **Encouraging Innovation:** Supporting research and development in space technologies and encouraging innovative approaches to solving the challenges of space exploration and colonization. Innovation drives progress and opens new frontiers for discovery.
- **Fostering Collaboration:** Building partnerships between governments, organizations, and individuals to advance space exploration and share knowledge and resources. Collaboration enhances our ability to achieve common goals and address global challenges.

Inspiration and education are key to building a future where humanity's cosmic legacy is characterized by exploration, discovery, and a commitment to ethical principles.

Envisioning the Future: A Cosmic Civilization

As we look to the future, we envision a cosmic civilization that reflects the highest aspirations and values of humanity. This vision involves:

- **A Thriving Space Community:** The establishment of vibrant and diverse space communities that contribute to the advancement of knowledge, culture, and technology.
- **Sustainable Practices:** The implementation of sustainable practices that ensure the long-term viability of space settlements and minimize our impact on the cosmos.
- **Ethical Principles:** The adherence to ethical principles that guide our actions and interactions with other life forms and celestial environments.

By pursuing this vision, we can create a cosmic legacy that is characterized by respect, responsibility, and a commitment to the well-being of all forms of life.

Conclusion: Leaving a Lasting Impact

Humanity's journey into the cosmos is a profound and transformative endeavor that will shape our legacy for generations to come. By embracing our aspirations, defining our legacy, and fulfilling our responsibilities, we can ensure that our cosmic endeavors contribute to a positive and lasting impact on the universe.

As we continue to explore and expand into space, let us do so with a sense of purpose and commitment to the highest values of humanity. Our cosmic legacy will be defined by the choices we make today and the impact we have on the future of our species and the universe.

Chapter 15 concludes.

Chapter 16: The Interplay of Science and Philosophy

Introduction

The relationship between science and philosophy is a profound and intricate one. As humanity ventures into space and explores the cosmos, the interplay between these two fields becomes increasingly significant. This chapter delves into how scientific discoveries and philosophical inquiry intersect, influence one another, and contribute to our understanding of the universe and our place within it.

The Role of Science in Shaping Philosophical Thought

Science, with its empirical methods and quest for understanding, has a substantial impact on philosophical thought. Key areas where science shapes the philosophy include:

- **Epistemology:** The study of knowledge and belief. Scientific advancements challenge and refine our understanding of what constitutes knowledge and how we acquire it. The discovery of new phenomena and the development of new technologies influence philosophical debates about the nature and limits of human knowledge.
- **Ontology:** The study of existence and reality. Scientific discoveries, such as the nature of space and time, the origins of the universe, and the complexity of life, prompt philosophical inquiries about the nature of reality. For

instance, the theory of relativity and quantum mechanics have led to philosophical discussions about the nature of time, space, and reality itself.

- **Ethics:** The study of moral principles. As science advances, it raises new ethical questions and challenges existing moral frameworks. Issues such as artificial intelligence, genetic modification, and space exploration introduce ethical dilemmas that require philosophical examination and guidance.
- **Metaphysics:** The study of fundamental questions about reality and existence. Scientific theories and discoveries often intersect with metaphysical questions, such as the nature of causality, determinism, and the nature of the universe. Philosophers engage with these questions to explore the implications of scientific findings on our understanding of existence.

Philosophy Informing Scientific Inquiry

Philosophy also plays a critical role in shaping scientific inquiry. Philosophical principles and methods influence the way scientific research is conducted and interpreted. Key areas where philosophy informs science include:

- **Scientific Method:** The philosophical foundations of the scientific method, including principles of logic, reasoning, and evidence, guide the practice of scientific research. Philosophers of science examine the nature of scientific reasoning, the structure of scientific theories, and the criteria for scientific explanation.

- **Conceptual Analysis:** Philosophy helps clarify and refine scientific concepts and theories. Philosophers engage in conceptual analysis to ensure that scientific concepts are well-defined, coherent, and consistent with empirical evidence. This process contributes to the development of rigorous and precise scientific theories.
- **Scientific Realism vs. Anti-Realism:** Philosophical debates about the nature of scientific theories and their relationship to reality influence scientific practice. Scientific realism asserts that scientific theories provide accurate descriptions of the world, while anti-realism questions the extent to which theories correspond to reality. These debates shape how scientists interpret and evaluate their findings.
- **Ethical Considerations:** Philosophy provides ethical frameworks for evaluating the implications of scientific research and technological advancements. Ethical principles guide decisions about the conduct of research, the application of scientific knowledge, and the responsible use of technology.

The Cosmic Perspective: A Philosophical Inquiry

The exploration of space and the cosmos invites profound philosophical questions and reflections. Key philosophical inquiries related to space exploration include:

- **The Meaning of Life:** Space exploration prompts existential questions about the meaning and purpose of human life. The search for extra-terrestrial life, the possibility of other habitable planets, and the quest for understanding the origins of the universe all contribute to philosophical reflections on the significance of human existence.

- **The Nature of Consciousness:** The exploration of space raises questions about the nature of consciousness and its relationship to the universe. Philosophical inquiries into the nature of consciousness, the mind-body problem, and the potential for extra-terrestrial intelligence intersect with scientific research in fields such as neuroscience, psychology, and astrobiology.
- **The Limits of Human Knowledge:** The vastness and complexity of the cosmos challenge our understanding of the limits of human knowledge. Philosophers and scientists grapple with questions about the extent to which we can comprehend the universe, the nature of cosmic knowledge, and the boundaries of human cognition.
- **The Ethical Implications of Space Exploration:** The ethical considerations of space exploration, including the potential impact on other forms of life, the preservation of celestial environments, and the responsible use of resources, raise philosophical questions about our moral obligations and responsibilities as cosmic explorers.

Integrating Science and Philosophy: A Unified Approach

To fully appreciate the interplay between science and philosophy, it is essential to adopt a unified approach that integrates both fields. This approach involves:

- **Interdisciplinary Collaboration:** Encouraging collaboration between scientists and philosophers to address complex questions and challenges. Interdisciplinary teams can provide comprehensive insights and solutions that bridge scientific and philosophical perspectives.

- **Holistic Understanding:** Adopting a holistic view that recognizes the interconnectedness of scientific and philosophical inquiry. A unified approach acknowledges that scientific discoveries and philosophical reflections are mutually informative and contribute to a deeper understanding of the universe.
- **Continuous Dialogue:** Fostering ongoing dialogue between science and philosophy to address emerging questions and challenges. Continuous engagement ensures that scientific advancements and philosophical insights remain aligned and mutually enriching.

Conclusion: The Journey of Discovery

The interplay between science and philosophy is a dynamic and enriching journey of discovery. As humanity explores the cosmos and advances its understanding of the universe, the collaboration between these two fields will continue to shape our knowledge, values, and aspirations. By integrating scientific inquiry with philosophical reflection, we can gain deeper insights into the nature of reality, the meaning of existence, and our place in the cosmos. This unified approach will guide us as we navigate the complexities of space exploration and contribute to the development of a more profound and comprehensive understanding of the universe.

Chapter 16 concludes.

Chapte Chpter 17
CHAPTER
CHAPTER
UNIED
Theory
THE UNITED THEORY

Chapter 17: The Ethical Dimensions of Cosmic Exploration

Introduction

As humanity continues to push the boundaries of space exploration, ethical considerations become increasingly critical. The vast expanse of space and the potential for encountering extra-terrestrial life raise profound moral questions and dilemmas. This chapter explores the ethical dimensions of cosmic exploration, examining the responsibilities and implications of our actions as we venture into the unknown.

Ethics of Space Exploration

Space exploration presents unique ethical challenges that require careful consideration and reflection. Key ethical dimensions include:

- **Responsibility to Preserve Celestial Environments:** As we explore and potentially colonize other planets and moons, we must consider the impact of our activities on these environments. The principle of environmental stewardship demands that we minimize our ecological footprint and avoid contaminating pristine extra-terrestrial landscapes.
- **Search for Extra-terrestrial Life:** The search for extra-terrestrial life raises ethical questions about how we should approach potential encounters. The discovery of alien life forms could have profound implications for our understanding

of life and our place in the universe. Ethical guidelines are needed to ensure that our interactions with extra-terrestrial life are respectful and responsible.

- **Planetary Protection:** Planetary protection involves preventing biological contamination of other planets and moons, as well as safeguarding Earth from potential contaminants brought back from space. Ethical considerations in planetary protection include the responsibility to avoid harming extra-terrestrial ecosystems and preventing the spread of harmful pathogens.

- **Resource Utilization:** The potential exploitation of space resources, such as mining asteroids or extracting resources from celestial bodies, raises ethical questions about the equitable distribution of these resources and the impact on space environments. We must consider the long-term consequences of resource utilization and the principles of fairness and justice in space exploration.

Ethical Frameworks for Space Exploration

Several ethical frameworks can guide our approach to space exploration:

- **Utilitarianism:** This framework evaluates the ethical implications of space exploration based on the overall benefits and harms to humanity. Utilitarianism emphasizes maximizing the well-being of the greatest number of people while minimizing potential negative consequences. In space exploration, utilitarian principles can guide decisions about the allocation of resources and the potential benefits of scientific discoveries.

- **Deontological Ethics:** Deontological ethics focuses on the moral duties and principles that govern our actions. In the context of space exploration, deontological ethics emphasize the importance of adhering to moral principles, such as respect for the autonomy of extra-terrestrial life forms and the duty to avoid harming celestial environments.
- **Virtue Ethics:** Virtue ethics emphasizes the development of moral character and virtues, such as courage, wisdom, and responsibility. In space exploration, virtue ethics encourages us to act with integrity, humility, and respect for the unknown. This approach highlights the importance of cultivating ethical virtues in the pursuit of cosmic discovery.
- **Eco-Centric Ethics:** Eco-centric ethics prioritize the intrinsic value of natural environments and ecosystems. This framework emphasizes the interconnectedness of all life forms and the need to protect and preserve the natural world. In space exploration, eco-centric ethics advocate for the responsible stewardship of celestial environments and the prevention of ecological harm.

Case Studies in Space Ethics

Examining specific case studies can provide insights into the ethical challenges and considerations of space exploration:

- **The Apollo Moon Landings:** The Apollo missions to the Moon raised questions about the potential impact of human activities on the lunar environment. The principles of planetary protection were considered to prevent contamination and preserve the integrity of the Moon's surface.

- **Mars Rover Missions:** The exploration of Mars by rovers has highlighted the importance of planetary protection and the need to prevent biological contamination. Ethical considerations include ensuring that Mars is not adversely affected by our exploration efforts and avoiding contamination of potential Martian habitats.
- **Asteroid Mining:** The prospect of mining asteroids for valuable resources presents ethical challenges related to the fair distribution of resources and the potential impact on space environments. The development of ethical guidelines for asteroid mining is essential to address these concerns.
- **Search for Extra-terrestrial Intelligence (SETI):** The search for extra-terrestrial intelligence involves the transmission of signals and messages into space. Ethical considerations include the potential risks of communicating with unknown civilizations and the responsibility to avoid harm.

International Collaboration and Governance

Effective international collaboration and governance are essential for addressing the ethical dimensions of space exploration:

- **International Agreements:** International agreements, such as the Outer Space Treaty and the Moon Agreement, establish principles and guidelines for the responsible use of outer space. These agreements provide a framework for addressing ethical issues and promoting cooperation among spacefaring nations.
- **Global Standards and Guidelines:** The development of global standards and guidelines for space exploration can help address ethical concerns and ensure that activities are conducted in a responsible and equitable manner.

Collaborative efforts among governments, space agencies, and scientific organizations are essential for establishing these standards.

- **Public Engagement and Transparency:** Engaging the public in discussions about the ethical implications of space exploration is crucial for ensuring transparency and accountability. Public input and involvement can help shape ethical guidelines and policies that reflect the values and concerns of society.

Conclusion: Navigating Ethical Frontiers

As humanity ventures further into space, navigating the ethical frontiers of cosmic exploration requires careful consideration and reflection. By addressing the ethical dimensions of space exploration and adopting responsible practices, we can ensure that our activities contribute to the greater good and reflect our commitment to moral principles.

The ethical challenges of space exploration invite us to consider our responsibilities as cosmic explorers and to strive for a harmonious balance between scientific advancement and ethical integrity. As we continue to explore the universe, let us embrace the opportunity to act with wisdom, respect, and responsibility.

Chapter 17 concludes.

Final Reflections from the Nebula Nexus

As we reach the end of this exploration, we stand on the cusp of understanding and mystery. The universe is an intricate dance of forces, matter, and energy, weaving together the vastness of the cosmos and the minuteness of particles. *Nebula Nexus* is not just a journey through stars and galaxies, but a contemplation of the deep connections between all levels of existence—between the infinitely small and the unfathomably large.

Through every chapter, we have ventured into the known and touched the edges of the unknown, realizing that there is always more to discover. Just like the nebulae that give birth to stars, the questions we ask today will fuel the discoveries of tomorrow.

Remember that you, too, are part of this cosmic web—connected to the stars, the galaxies, and the mysteries that stretch far beyond our sight. The more we seek, the more we realize that we are both explorers and creations of the very forces that shape the universe.

Thank you for joining me on this voyage through the nebulae, stars, and cosmic webs. The universe is vast, and our journey has just begun.

Acknowledgements

This book would not have been possible without the unwavering support and inspiration of those around me. To my family and friends, your encouragement gave me the strength to push forward and explore the unknown. To my readers, thank you for sharing in this journey of discovery—I hope these pages have sparked your curiosity about the cosmos, just as writing them has deepened mine.

About the Author

Knox, a pseudonym chosen for its resonance across cultures, is a passionate explorer of the cosmos and a seeker of answers to the universe's biggest questions. Through writing, Knox blends the scientific and the philosophical, offering readers a fresh perspective on the infinite complexity of the universe. *Nebula Nexus* is the culmination of years spent gazing at the stars and contemplating the unseen connections between all things.

www.ingramcontent.com/pod-product-compliance
Lightning Source LLC
Chambersburg PA
CBHW040802120726
48005CB00012B/1278